COUNTRY NEIGHBORHOOD

THE MACMILLAN COMPANY
NEW YORK · BOSTON · CHICAGO · DALLAS
ATLANTA · SAN FRANCISCO
MACMILLAN AND CO., LIMITED
LONDON · BOMBAY · CALCUTTA · MADRAS
MELBOURNE
THE MACMILLAN COMPANY
OF CANADA, LIMITED
TORONTO

COUNTRY NEIGHBORHOOD

By ELIZABETH *Jane* COATSWORTH

With decorations by Hildegard Woodward

THE MACMILLAN COMPANY · NEW YORK

1944

A WARTIME BOOK

Printed in the United States of America

The decorations throughout this book are not of actual houses in this particular neighborhood, but represent types often found in Maine.

COUNTRY NEIGHBORHOOD

Our farm lies on the east slope of a point—or, as it is here called, a neck—stretching out into one of the three terminal bays of Taniscot Pond. There are three farms on Hill's Neck, and ours, the middle one, lies like the others in the midst of hayfields overlooking the water with pasture land above, largely overgrown now; beyond that, woodland stretches down to Green Cove on the west. The neighborhood is entirely farming: the farms are not rich, for the soil is not rich. The handful of cows, the yard of chickens produce more cash than the rocky acres of thin earth. The old agricultural industry is discouraged: it no longer pays to plant wheat and barley, oats, or rye. Only occasionally is a field resown to clover, or an experiment in millet hazarded, or a couple of acres planted to fodder corn. The population has shrunk, and the woods are webbing in the corners of the fields: old cellar holes and lost orchards and gravestones among the pines bear testimony to this.

But the people on this back road which is almost impassable in mud time retain the old independent self-respecting Yankee tradition. While here and there the blood has run out and families like plants have gone to seed, the men and women of our township are for the most part people of character and breeding, not cut out of any one pattern as by machinery, but whittled and showing the grain. Among them you will find some of the oldest names in the history of New England, mixed with the names of the Germans who settled in the neighboring town of Knoxboro in the mid-eighteenth century. Our road with its small weather-beaten farms has in the last few years taken on a new hopefulness, that fundamental and basic hopefulness of birth. One day we counted thirty-six children in its scattered farms where twenty years ago there were only two along its three miles; for the Hill's Neck Road is of course only a side road starting at the Hillsboro post office and running to our gate, where it changes into a lane for us and the Hill farm, then into a wood road, and so veins out into dim trails leading to the water.

Our town is a very scattered one. Only the post office, one store, a church, the small anonymous town office building, a school, three or four houses, and an obelisk to Daniel Hill beside the old village pump, mark its nucleus. Many people drive through it without suspecting that they have gone through a town at all; but it is an old town for Maine, settled in the eighteenth century as soon as the French and Indian wars were over. For a wonder we are not on a river, like most of our neighbor towns which grew up at the head of navigation on the great salt rivers which lie like arrows in a quiver, side by side: the St. George, the Medomac, the Damariscotta, the Sheepscott, the Kennebec, beautiful rivers with beautiful names. Sprinkled in the rivers and along the shores are innumerable islands, and inland there are innumerable lakes. So that even here in the farming country we see the sea gulls coasting along the old pasture lands looking for blueberries in July, and watch the sea haze blow in and hang upright on our horizon. On damp days when the wind is southeasterly, we can occasionally hear the foghorn at Pocassett Point, and in the old barn of the farm next door someone long ago carved on a beam the outline of a schooner under full sail. To either side of Hillsboro were ship-building and ship-sailing towns, though on our own road few of the men seem to have gone to sea. It is rather to the woods that the farmers' imaginations turn, and as surely as fall comes the young men oil their guns to go see if they can get them a deer, perhaps in their own wood lot but preferably farther off. With a tent or an old trailer they start out for the back country with a friend or two for company. They wear checked wool shirts, trousers laced in at the knee, high boots, and long red wool socks. The expedition is always a success, whether they bring back a deer or not, for they like the return to the pioneer conditions of their ancestors, and now they have new stories to tell around the stove.

Chapter 2

THE FIRST kitchen which we have come to know well is that of our nearest neighbors the Hardys. He is an old man with a fine massive head, slow of speech, his back bent. She is as brisk as he is deliberate, always smiling, always stirring something, or looking in at an oven door which lets out smells of gingerbread or pie. They are old, and their daughter is married and lives on the main road. They support each other like two aged trees with intertwined branches. If Mr. Hardy is dipping the bills of newly arrived chicks in buttermilk, Mrs. Hardy in her apron with a man's shapeless felt hat on her white hair is beside him helping to dip. When he is getting in the hay it is she who leads the old horse twenty feet straight out from the barn door and then back again, hoisting up the load into the loft instead of pitching it up as they still do in French Canada.

And when she is washing, Mr. Hardy stands in the shed and wrings out the heavy clothes for her and takes them out to hang on the line. If the cows are obstinate at finding their places in the tie-up he can curse them blackly. For more than fifty years she has disliked his habit of chewing tobacco and spitting in the stove. He riles her too by his suggestions that perhaps she has not remembered her manners: "Of course I've asked them for supper,

Walter! They can't stay. But here, you take some of this spice cake along with you. 'Tisn't very good, but it's my mother's old recipe."

The Hardys' kitchen has dim flowered wallpaper, a sink with a pump, a big wood stove with a hot-water tank beside the wood box, two or three chairs, a round table in the corner by the pantry door, which is set for the next meal and covered with a fresh newspaper, and an old sofa in the warm corner beside the stove, where Mr. Hardy rests his back or the cat brings her kittens. There is always a cat with well-behaved kittens, as surely as there is a Star of Bethlehem plant hanging in one of the windows, usually showing purple or white flowers, for Mrs. Hardy has the green thumb.

After supper any evening except Saturday, when the Hardys take their baths in the kitchen, they are glad to have visitors. In summer they sit in the woodshed looking south through the wide doorway down the road across the Heath to the lights of the Sherman farm. The cat often comes and sits on the wood block to be near them, and we are likely to refuse their kindly bustle after more chairs, and to drop instead onto the low step which leads to the summer kitchen. There is a pleasant smell of split wood, and grass beyond the threshold, but in the dusk we can scarcely see one another's faces. The talk is best on fall and winter nights in the lamplighted kitchen about the stove, when it is shut in upon itself and is not dissipated by the evening wind, the rising of the moon, or the cry of an owl.

"You know," begins Mrs. Hardy, "there used to be a witch across on the other side of the pond. Folks on our side weren't often superstitious, but on the other side of the pond queer things happened. This Tildy Tripp was dead by the time I came along, but when I was a child I knew lots of people who had known her. She lived in a house on the upper road which is still standing, though after she died no one liked to live in it because of the noises and the way doors slammed when there wasn't any wind. She used to be neighborly with the family that lived in the farm with the big barn right across from here. Well, one day she was coming down the road when a couple of men were plowing with a yoke of oxen. I don't know if you know what the clevis pin is, but it's the iron pin that fastens the yoke to the plow. As she was going by, the clevis pin dropped out, and of course the plowing had to stop while the men hunted for it.

"Tildy was quite a distance off, going down the road all the time, and she went on to the house to sit in the kitchen. The men hunted and hunted. A clevis pin is big, and it seemed as though it couldn't hide itself away like that. Finally they got mad and came down to the house. One of them went over to where Tildy was sitting talking.

" 'Here, Tildy, none of your tricks. You give me back that clevis pin if you know what's good for you! I've got to get on with my plowing.'

"She looked up at him as innocent as you please.

" 'Why, you know perfectly well I wasn't ever near your old clevis pin,' she says, 'I wasn't even within fifty feet of it.'

"But he wasn't to be put off. He raised the oxgoad he had in his hand.

" 'You give it to me or you'll be sorry,' he said, and that settled it.

" 'Well, well,' she says, taking the pin from under her

apron. 'Take it, take it, and stop raising such a hullabaloo over nothing.'

"Another time at the same farm the woman found that all her young geese were taking sick of something. They'd go around a day or two pining, and then they'd die. She got tired of seeing it. Maybe she and Tildy Tripp had had words, or maybe it was after the clevis-pin quarrel. Anyway, the next morning she saw one of those young goslings looking peaked, she split it right open with an ax and laid it on the hot stove, open side down. It must have sizzled there five minutes or more. Afterwards she heard from someone who had been at Tildy's house at that time that Tildy let out a kind of shriek and walked up and down holding her hands to her stomach and complaining of the dreadful searing pains she had. Pretty soon she was all right again, but no more geese in that neighborhood ever took sick."

We must have looked our questions, for Mrs. Hardy shook her head with a little smile.

"I don't know. Nothing like that ever happened our side of the pond."

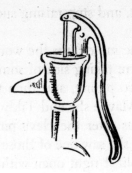

Chapter 3

"HOUSES HAVE very definite feelings," Mrs. Livingston said, looking down from the overgrown brick terrace towards the river. "Now this little house is just beginning to care whether people come back to it or not. For years after we found it abandoned and brought it here, it didn't care whether it was lived in or wasn't. But this spring when I came back it had for the first time an air of expectancy. It is beginning to recover from being transplanted."

"I've sometimes felt a definite good will or ill will about houses," I said, thinking of the Hingham house which has so strongly the mellow eighteenth century acceptance of life—and of death, too.

But I spoke of another house, a very small one with two peaked gables painted a pale green and buried in the woods on a point of land between two branches of the Sheepscott River, so isolated and so lost that nothing is left to it of its former fields and pastures but a handkerchief-sized lawn behind a trimmed arborvitae hedge and two window boxes of petunias in mysterious bloom. For years we called it the House of the Three Bears. We discovered it by crossing a condemned bridge, passing at long intervals three houses, one haunted, and so beyond the third house after a mile of lane, under line pine trees which met over-head, coming straight into this small domain with its air of reserved secrecy. It was never occupied, nor was there the slightest sign of any human being about the place; but the hedge was cut, the lawn smooth, the petunias in bloom.

Years later we met the owner. As we talked of the house her eyes grew tender, and she stretched out her left hand.

"You see I don't wear an engagement ring," she said. "The house was my engagement ring. We only come to it now for a week or two in a summer. But it is a strange place. It has a blessing upon it. Whoever lives in it is made whole again. Men have come there wounded after the war, women worn out with sickness, young couples newly mar-ried, older couples losing their way in life, and always they have left the house reassured and well again. I don't un-derstand it myself, but it has never failed yet."

"Most houses deep in the woods are inclined to be melancholy," I said to Mrs. Livingston, recalling this earlier talk with her friend. But she smiled and shook her head.

"Not that little house," she agreed. "Mine in the city hasn't the healing gift, but it is very eager for its own. After the family was grown up and scattered it was closed for a good many years, and when I came back to it I meant to sell it, for it was much larger than I needed; but it kept willing me to come back so hard that I had to give in, and I've lived there ever since."

The conversation went on to other things, but a corner of my mind stayed with houses, with bad and melancholy houses which disliked the families under their roofs; with empty houses whose despair was an almost visible presence in their rooms where the torn shades sucked in and out against a broken windowpane; with the malevolence of new-built houses which have not yet been broken into service.

My Aunt Nellie for years circumvented my uncle's desire to buy land and build.

"As surely as he does it, he'll die," she assured me.

Our family had almost no superstitions. We broke mirrors, watched people out of sight, and spilled salt without a qualm. But Aunt Nellie was sure that no elderly person was safe in a new house.

Henry has told me that he knew the superstition as a boy in New England, and that it was then still an occasional practice for an elderly couple to hire young people to live in a new house for a month or so to take off the curse which their fresh vitality was strong enough to offset.

When I reached home I went to the kitchen to consult Grace. She stopped mixing her excellent mayonnaise to nod.

"Lots of people still think that," she said. "Yes, you can get young people to live in a new house first. Or some people think it helps to build some old boards into the ell or old bricks into the chimney." She whirred the beater reflectively and paused again. "Then there's others say it's enough to throw in through the door ahead of you a broom, some bread, and a bag of salt," she concluded.

Chapter 4

HERE IN OUR country much of the old agricultural cycle has been lost. The husking bees and house-raisings are over. I have never heard of the community's bringing wood to the minister's woodshed, or of the women paring and stringing apple chips to dry in a long evening together of work and laughter. But certain things survive. Between the haying and the season for chopping wood for the winter there is a halcyon time, from late August through September, when the farmers expect to enjoy themselves. Then come the church suppers, from the humble baked-bean suppers at thirty-five cents to the wonderful chicken suppers and even wild-game suppers whose tickets cost a dollar. We all—when we have gas—run the countryside; everyone milks his cows, lets the dog loose, puts out the fire in the stove and locks up the empty farmhouse. From the oldest man bent on his stick to the newborn goggle-eyed baby, the family piles into the car and is off. We range far for a church supper, eat enormously in a silence only broken by "Pass me the chocolate cake, please," or "What's that over there—blueberry pie?" and hurry to give

[11]

our seats to the people waiting at the door, while the women of the parish in their aprons scurry up and down the long tables, carrying more food and huge pots of coffee, usually in the yellow light of big kerosene lamps suspended from the ceiling.

But church suppers do not exhaust our entertainments. We have also the fairs. There are usually three or four fairs in reach of every family, though they may not go to them all, having their favorites here as with the suppers. These small village fairs are a mixture as old as New England of the professional and the amateur; a meeting of the farm boy with the slick and hardened barker, acrobat, and horse racer. For several days before a fair the grounds show a seasonal activity. The roads are then charming to travel, with here a huge truck going by loaded with the parts of a merry-go-round or swings, and there a pair or even two pair of oxen deliberately swinging along half off the black asphalt, their driver walking beside them. Or a horse truck will pass with the thin twitching ears of a trotting horse high against the sky, and then there are the trailers where the concessionaires live, sometimes even a gypsy trailer with children staring out at you from black opaque eyes. Later come the old farm cars with fruits, quilts, and crates of hens and roosters for the exhibition hall. The woman beside the driver may be balancing a basket of jelly glasses on her knees. Everyone looks anxious and pleased at the same time. Later as you pass the grounds such blares of music, baaing of lambs, mooing of cattle, and shouting of voices greet you that you would be indifferent indeed if you could go by.

I remember that one year the small Scotch minister who was then preaching at the Hillsboro Church on alternate

Sundays came to see us. The Taniscot Fair was just over, and he said that he always enjoyed it and went every year to talk with the itinerant performers and preach to them the word of God.

"They are always very interested to hear what I have to say," he assured us. "They all seem to take it quite to heart."

But he was a very honest man, and his conscience weighed what he had just said and found it wanting a little.

"All but the mermaid," he amended.

Mr. Hardy has his own memories of the fair. One evening when we were all sitting in the kitchen he asked Mrs. Hardy if she remembered the time there was a horse whose head was where his tail ought to be.

She nodded but let him tell the story.

"They had a tent rigged up with a sign 'Ten cents to see the Horse with his Head where his Tail ought to be,' and after a while people began paying to go in. They didn't stay long and came out laughing, but none of them would tell what was inside that tent. And people got curious and a lot of them paid to go in. I did myself. And do you know what they had in there? Well, they had just an ordinary old horse in a stall with his tail to the manger and his head to the open part of the stall. They hadn't told a lie. He had his tail where his head ought to be all right."

"I didn't go in," said Mrs. Hardy. "I never could abide freaks. But I remember your telling me about it at the time."

Chapter 5

THE SHERMANS' kitchen is usually filled with people, just as the barn door and the shed door ranged parallel to the kitchen door are likely to be filled with cats and their kittens. The house hasn't been painted for years and has the silvery moth-wing look which I am very fond of. The two great elms darkening the seldom-used front door are not marriage trees as I supposed, but rather birthday trees, and were planted for old Mr. Sherman's two sisters, who are still alive and although old themselves drive their car occasionally down the Hill's Neck Road for a visit. "How fast trees grow in Maine!" as someone said to me only yesterday. "People talk about growth in the tropics, but these short Maine summers force the trees as fast as any tropics."

Certainly to look at the elms intertwining their branches high above the roofs of the buildings you would say that they had stood there for more than a hundred years. Well, after all, they have been there a long time.

We climb two steep steps and rap at the screen door which is often "buttoned," as people say in these parts, to keep it from blowing open in the wind. The kitchen is almost square, and its remarkable feature is its floor with narrow boards laid in concentric squares about a single small square of black cherry wood in its very center. There have never been rugs or linoleum on the floor; a thousand scrubbings have worn it smooth and soft-grained. The window over the sink looks out across the Heath and its sluggish stream. As fall comes on, Mrs. Sherman reports the deer, foxes, and moose that she sees from this window; but at other times of the year she can tell you with accuracy every car and person who has passed along the road and the hour at which they went by—a faculty which is a great help to us when we are trying to trace who it was who came to call when we were out, or what light truck drove by late in the evening, turned about, and drove away without stopping.

Mrs. Sherman is a very handsome, straight-standing woman, a good deal younger than Mr. Sherman, with his drooping white mustache and his eyes so blue and humorous in his tanned face.

Laura, before she married Norman, the Shermans' only son, was in our household for several years, so she seems part of the family, with her rosy face and easy laugh. She is almost always in the kitchen with Mrs. Sherman and the two little boys, one still a baby. At present Norman is home, not working at the Shipyards as he has done for nearly two years now. Two of his ribs are mending after a fall from a scaffolding, and here is one of those curious coincidences which seem to occur more often in the country than in the city. Norman broke his ribs a year to a day from the time that his father fell off the hay-mow last summer and broke his. There was a woman hereabouts who was twice married, and each of her husbands was blinded in one eye by an accident with barbed wire. We used to see her, and she had a sad look as though she couldn't understand how such an unusual thing could have happened twice over to her. But here strangeness is more accepted than among people who constantly read other men's ideas and are more closely gripped in the world of machinery. When Henry tells about his dream of a chimney fire and of meeting Mrs. Kimball in a car with some of her family in a great state of unsettledness, and about telling Grace and me of his dream twenty-four hours before the Kimball house caught fire at the chimney and burned into the cellar—no one is at all surprised, nor offers the slightest rationalized explanation. Here the isolated families fighting their separate fights against Fate and the encroaching wilderness are aware of curious recurrences and accept them.

Although work is hard on the Sherman farm with Mr. Sherman growing old, and Mrs. Sherman not very strong, and Norman away most of the day, and the chicken yard to be attended to and the eggs to be gathered, weighed, and packed, and the little boys to be taken care of, the Sherman kitchen is a very jolly place. The whole family dearly loves a joke, and loves to laugh and to sing. Mr. Sherman tells us sometimes of the old days, of his grandfather who brought his wife into the wilderness on horseback about 1800, and built a log cabin between the two old apple trees which still look over the Heath, where only the well remains, covered with a great stone. Or he will tell of early days at the sawmill at the head of the bay where fifty teams of oxen would come in a row hauling lumber down the ice, or of the other well he climbed down into as a boy, from which he could see a star at midday, or of the raccoon his mother baked, which tasted so good until he knew what it was.

"Why is the place where the water drains into the Heath called Witch Bridge?" I asked one day. "Was there a witch?"

Mr. Sherman's face lighted up reminiscently.

"Well, when we all were children we used to stay up at the end of the road pretty late. Wouldn't get home until after dark. Mother used to tell us to come home, but you know how children are. So one evening we were coming along late as usual. You know it's pretty lonely in that stretch with the bushes growing close on one side of the road and the Heath stretching out on the other. It was pretty dark, just bright enough to see things still, when all of a sudden something big and white came out of the bushes waving its arms at us. The hair rose right up on our heads, and we ran home in a hurry, I tell you. Mother wasn't in, but she came in soon after with her sewing bag over her arm. Said she'd been up at my aunt's across the road. We children never thought that was funny. We had so much to tell her about the witch that had chased us. She just nodded and nodded and said, 'Dear me,' and 'Gracious.' She didn't even tell us we'd better never go on that road again in the dark. But you can bet we were home for meals on time after that. It was years before any of us would cross Witch Bridge after the sun had gone down." And Mr. Sherman and all the family laugh appreciatively.

"My mother was a wonderful woman," he adds. "When she died we gave up cooking in the open fireplace. We bricked it up just as it was, with the andirons and the crane and the big hanging pot all in their places. They must be there to this day, in case anyone ever wants to use them again."

Chapter 6

THE GRAHAMS were the first people to settle on the Hill's Neck Road after the Hills who built the big house next to us at the very end of the Neck, sometime about the end of the eighteenth century. I never remember that, without being overwhelmed by the magnanimity of the human spirit which would build on so large and civilized a scale in the midst of bears and Indians; and not only did they build this great house with its many windows and fine doors, but they changed their minds about its location and moved it across the ice one winter and up the steep slope from the water to the commanding position it now holds. I wonder how many yoke of oxen were used and who drove them, and how they knew how to do it? But in Maine moving things boldly has always been a characteristic of the people. They say that the old German church at Knoxboro was stolen one winter's night from the north side of the river and set up again on the south side where it still stands, although the north-siders must have been pretty mad about it for the first thirty or forty years. The Marie Antoinette house of Wiscasset was also moved across the wide Sheepscott in its time, and I have heard a tale of a good-sized schooner having been built well inland to be near the supply of white oaks, and then taken to the water in the grand manner with oxen.

But the Grahams did not move their low early nineteenth century house. It was built where it now stands, though Mrs. Graham tells me that the first log cabin stood near the barn on the other side of the brook.

"He must have settled where he did account of the running water. Maybe that's why we find Indian things on our farm more than most places. There's not much running water hereabouts. Probably that's what made that Indian who called himself Bedagi ask if he could camp here. Didn't you ever hear of him? It was when Keith was a little boy. He says those Indians were real good people. They wouldn't even pick up an apple off the ground without asking if they might. That must have been sixty or more years ago. The schoolhouse at the Bremens' was used then of course, and the Indian children went to school there, a boy and a girl. There was a little one, too, who died while they were here and was buried up in the corner of the graveyard. No, there wasn't a real stone, but I know the place. Haven't you ever heard of the entertainment Bedagi gave at the schoolhouse one evening? All the mothers and fathers of the pupils came—I guess anyone who wanted to, for that matter—and his little boy stood up across the room with an apple on his head, and Bedagi shot it off with an arrow. Then the little girl lay right down on the floor and there before everyone's eyes he threw knives around her and outlined her from head to heels. Gracious, I'm glad I wasn't there to see it."

Gentle Mrs. Graham, hardly taller than the cosmos which flowers everywhere for her! She has had four children, a daughter who lives at home and three sons now all grown up and away; but she seems like a little girl herself, unhardened by life. To her, birds and flowers are still the most important things she knows. She writes verses and gives people things: she walks the stony Maine roads to go neighboring, as it is called, always with a box of berries or a packet of flower seeds in her hand, or maybe some cookies she has just made, or a pincushion she has put together out of some silk she came across. In a part of the world where everyone is generous, Mrs. Graham shines as the most generous of all, giving, giving, giving as naturally as a cricket chirrups or a chipmunk runs on a sunny wall. Because we had been talking of Indians, Mrs. Graham wanted to give me a little string of wampum which had been found near here. It was the only local wampum I have ever seen, and I failed in an equal generosity of acceptance. I could not bring myself to take more than three or four beads from one end. Only saints can give and take as freely as the elements come and go.

Chapter 7

"IF SHE COULD BE stiff, I could be stout," declares Grace,
outlining with relish an interview with a high-handed
woman who had stopped to inquire the way and seemed
inclined to hold Grace responsible for having lost it. Grace
has recently become a great-grandmother; but it will be
several years before she is seventy, and her hair has hardly
a gray streak in it, and her eyes snap as brightly and her
lips lie as firm and ready as they must have when
she was a young girl. She is stouthearted and stout of body
as well, with that thickness which so often means vitality
and a hold on life—a short, vigorous, red-cheeked woman
whose presence brings life into a house as wind and sun
bring it, and as noisily too sometimes as the wind. She
scolds the children, bandies words with the deliverymen,
and stands no nonsense from telephone operators. She is
ripe with experience; no human sorrow or joy but she has
tasted it and is willing to taste it again. She has known
poverty and disappointment, but she is eager for each new
day, watching every bird which moves in the apple tree
beyond the windows over her sink, and hungry for flowers.
She knows everything which happens in the countryside.
In five minutes' idle chat by the door she has learned what
every man, woman, and child and animal on our road has

been up to during the last month. She sees life in its tragedy and comedy, like an old actress who knows all the roles. And to fit with her observations she has a rich and old-fashioned vocabulary full of adages which we have never heard before.

"The new broom sweeps clean, but the old one knows where the dirt lies."

"She'll tie a knot with her tongue, she can't untie with her hands."

"What is allotted, can't be blotted."

"Better an empty house than a bad tenant."

Or "Promises are like piecrust—easily broken." So the stories she tells are enriched and made universal with the wisdom of her mother and grandmothers.

Grace is a Nova Scotian brought up in Halifax, on her mother's side from a line of United Loyalists who came there from Florida rather than take the oath of allegiance to the new government of the United States. There were two brothers named Lowe, and they owned a "block of marble houses in Brier Lane in London"; but they left them to their sisters and went to the new world. One had a sawmill and one a flour mill in Pensacola, and the money they earned they kept in crocks in their closets. But though they loved the new country they were British and would take no oath except to the King, when the territory passed to the United States early in the nineteenth century.

When Grace's mother was a little girl a great-aunt used to visit at their farm. She was the last alive of the emigrants who had left Florida so long ago. She had been twelve at the time the difficult decision had been made. They might leave unmolested but they were not allowed to carry any money with them. So the men buried the crocks of coins by night in a place where they still must be, since no one in the family remembers where it was, and the women sat up until dawn taking out the lead from the cloth buttons worn in such numbers at that time, and replacing it with gold pieces and sewing the precious buttons back again up and down the men's coats and vests so that the family might carry at least a little security with them into the new home so far to the north. And that was what the great-aunt would describe to Grace's mother, remembering the room where her mother and she, still a child, sat sewing hour by hour by a candle while their tears fell, and the pile of buttons on the table grew larger.

Grace shakes her head and sighs.

"But Nova Scotia was a cold, poor land," she says, "and the old people soon died and the young ones went down in the world. It was not a place where they could thrive."

Chapter 8

Grace lives a life of marvel. The cat which her daughter got from the Hardy farm next door has not had a life like other cats. I saw him as a kitten, a big fluffy deep golden ball with all four of his paws double. I have never seen him grown up with his heavy coat and sweeping tail, but I know what a fierce hunter he is, and how he will leap and catch a ball five feet in the air. I know too what a baby he is, accustomed to a great deal of attention, and how he will come when his mistress blows a whistle, leaping over back fences and streaking across back yards, startling anyone whom he may pass. But the other day when Grace spoke about the time Ginger brought back the diamond, I was surprised.

"We were in the kitchen," Grace explained, "when Ginger came in limping. He'd apparently got something stuck in the soft hair around the pads of one of his hind feet, and he sat down on the linoleum and stuck his foot out and began pulling at it with his teeth in that way cats do. Pretty soon something dropped out and Jenny went over to see what had been bothering him.

" 'Why, look at that,' she said. 'It looks like a diamond.' So when Dan came back from work she said to him, 'Look at the piece of glass Ginger brought home in his foot.'

" 'Glass!' said Dan who once worked for a jeweler. 'That's not glass, that's a diamond.' "

To make sure he took it into Boston and had it tested. It was a diamond all right. Jenny put an advertisement in the Lost and Found column of the local paper, but no one ever answered it; so some day she's going to have it cut in two and add a small diamond to each side of the one in her engagement ring.

"That's a cat worth having," said I.

If Ginger is a cat worth having, he's not the only cat who has brought money to his mistress. Half the farm-houses of our neighborhood have Maine shags playing about the sheds and barn doors, and the women make a little money from the sale of kittens, which are col-lected and sent down to pet shops in Boston and other cities. The prevailing rate of pay at the farmhouse steps is two dollars for a girl kitten and three for a boy, though a fine white kitten with blue eyes may come as high as five dollars. No one knows where these "shags" or "coon-cats" originally came from, though Wiscasset claims that the captain who tried to rescue Marie Antoinette, and who sailed home instead with only a hold filled with palace fur-niture, was the very man who on another voyage brought back a pair of Persian cats, from whom all the long-haired cats of Maine are sprung. Maybe so. At any rate they are thoroughly at home here, and live hardy little-cared-for lives, though often they retain the look of palace cats as they walk the stone walls in search of chipmunks, or sit in a sunny corner of a tumble-down barn.

There is an old story from Westport Island of a cat—whether long- or short-haired—which kept a family alive during starvation times with the man away fighting the

British, by bringing back icefish from an open place in the ice of the Sheepscott River where a spring flowed up. Many a cat has brought back rats—why not "icefish," whatever an "icefish" may be? Certainly last fall we became acquainted with a very gentle gold shag. The weather had turned cold with heavy frost over the fields in the mornings, and when the loons swam in our cove they left two widening lines behind them of skim ice. We were saving gasoline as was everybody else, so we went out little and had few visitors. One day as I walked down our lane to see what deer had crossed it in the early morning, I noticed a thin yellow cat with a very fine feathery tail hunting in the field. I didn't call to it, thinking it must belong to one of the neighboring farms, though it was wandering rather far from home; but that afternoon it came to our shed.

Near by we could see that it was almost starved to death. For a week we fed it continually. Like most Maine cats it would eat anything, cereal, bread and milk, table scraps—anything; but for a long time this poor cat could not be filled. It was very gentle and well-mannered, never showing the slightest greediness, starved as it was. It was altogether at ease with Pug, although Pug regarded it with some mistrust. We named it Yellow Brother, I think. At that time the chief heat of the farm came from a big ornate stove in the dining room which we called Lillian Russell and which kept warm all night on coal. Pug had his wicker basket beside the stove, but when Yellow Brother would step into it Pug would step out instantly, looking thoroughly disgruntled. I remember on that first evening I found in the shed a carton, rather small and high-sided, into which I wedged a small sofa cushion. For anyone as flexible as a cat, it would do very well temporarily. I remember the scene when we took out the lamp, with Pug on his cushion in his dog basket on one side of Lillian Russell, and Yellow Brother blandly slant-eyed in his box on the other.

But how different was the scene when Henry called me to see it next morning! Now it was the cat which stretched at its ease in the basket as though upon display, and the black, wrinkled and disgusted face of Pug which appeared in the box where he lay wedged tight between its four sides. He had to be pulled out, as a cork is pulled out of a bottle, and we could never guess how Pug—who is nothing of a climber—had ever got into the carton without knocking it over.

We began asking about our guest and letting it be known at the grocery that a stray cat had come to us, and one evening an old Ford hammered up to the door in the darkness, and a woman in the slacks and button of a worker at the Ironworks appeared in the doorway and asked almost fiercely—

"Have you got my cat?"

I stood my ground.

"What color is it?"

"Yellow."

Then I led her to the kitchen, and in a moment more she had Yellow Brother in her arms.

"I thought he had been poisoned. They was poisoning rats around an empty house just below us," she said. She wanted to pay me for our care of him.

"What's his name?" I asked.

Her face took on a slight look of embarrassment.

"Baby," she said.

Together we fitted together Baby's adventure. That

[27]

fall he had been bringing up a litter of little half-brothers and sisters in the shed, a year younger than he was. And then one day they had all been sold to the cat dealer. Baby had disappeared that evening. He had gone to look for them. He had looked for them for three weeks, through the woods and fields, apparently almost without food. And when he could look no farther he had come to us.

Among the rather devil-may-care cats of Maine, Baby had the gentlest spirit I have ever met with.

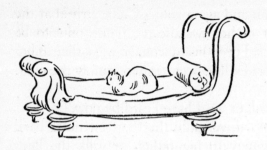

Chapter 9

Grace's mother was a country girl who lived in a white farmhouse with twin gables, surrounded by a white picket fence. There was a great white birch by the door, and a brook ran through the farmyard. The farm stood fourteen miles from Halifax, but Grace's mother, who was also named Grace, thought nothing of walking to town and back in a day. She was a vigorous, red-cheeked, black-eyed, black-haired girl with plenty of suitors among the sons of the neighboring farmers; but her heart was given to a young man from the town whose father was a tailor with ten men working under him, and whose mother had been the daughter of a British colonel, and never forgot the fact. She, proud woman, could not endure the idea of her only son's marrying a farmer's daughter, and was no doubt relieved when he determined to join the Union troops to help to drive slavery from the continent. One wonders how many fiery young Canadians were to be found fighting for liberty in those long seesaw Virginia battles? At all events young Grace kissed her lover good-by, and they swore to be true to each other and to write often, and to be married when he returned from his crusade.

In those days there was of course no Rural Free Delivery, and the letters to Grace were to be sent to Halifax in his mother's care. Again and again young Grace arrived at the unwelcoming door of her sweetheart's house only to be told that no word had been heard from Jim. Neither to her nor to his mother had a line been written, grimly the older woman said.

"He must be dead, or we'd have heard by now."

And Grace would drive sadly the fourteen miles back in the market wagon with her father, or walk the long lonely road if her anxiety had sent her there alone.

When months and then years had gone by and still no word had reached her, even Grace was forced to believe that Jim was dead.

"You can't live an old maid forever, waiting for a dead man," one of her country suitors pressed her. "I know you loved Jim, but if we get married you'll come to love me, too."

Grace said, "If Jim came back I'd marry him in a minute."

"If," said the suitor. "But poor Jim isn't coming back."

So young Grace walked to Halifax one fine summer day in 1865 with a friend who was to be her bridesmaid at the wedding that evening. They were buying their bonnets for the occasion, these lively girls who could walk twenty-eight miles and then dance half the night! I imagine that Grace's feelings must have been mixed as she gazed into the milliner's mirror and chose her bonnet, surely one with pink roses about the face. Then with their boxes over their arms the two girls started for home. Some miles out of town they saw a man in uniform walking along ahead of them, going in the same direction. His whistling came back to them, "When Johnny comes marching home."

You know the rest. It was Jim on his way to find his

Grace. He was alive and well, and just in time to circumvent his mother's dishonorable schemes. Somewhere in the universe blew the white ashes of what had once been his letters to Grace, burned by his mother. But all was well which ended well. There was a wedding that very evening, and the bonnets were worn and the girls danced; but it was Jim who married Grace.

The story had a long patient sequel. The tailor speculated, and his comfortable fortune was all lost in a day. The shop, the ten little tailors, and the good house in Halifax disappeared like a dream. Jim's two sisters who had had all the advantages of travel, music, and French, and who were now married, offered no help. It was Jim and Grace who took the old people in for the rest of their lives. The tailor was merry and kind.

"If you've lost your money you haven't it to worry about," he would say, and wink at his grandchildren. But his wife, who had been a British colonel's daughter, behaved as though her daughter-in-law's house and her daughter-in-law's children were beneath her notice. Her husband too was included in her quarrel with life. For weeks at a time she would say no word to any of them beyond a cold "Good morning," at the beginning of the day. Only to her son would she talk. Our Grace remembered her in her silk dress with a small white apron over her knees sitting bolt upright all day long by the window reading the Halifax journals. Never did she offer to help in the work of that busy household, never did she laugh or play with even the youngest grandchild. When an old acquaintance would send her a barrel of fine apples she would keep it for herself, beyond a grudging plateful for the table when the barrel was first opened.

And all that time Grace, her daughter-in-law, dealt patiently and lovingly with her year after year, and no word of reproach was ever spoken.

"She's Jim's mother, and that's enough," she would say when her friends expostulated.

At last came the old woman's final illness. Her husband had died some years before, and now Grace nursed her as she had nursed him, patiently day and night. Jim sent word to his sisters, and they arrived bag and baggage, stayed for a day or two, made their last farewells to their mother, and left again, not waiting for her to die. It was Grace who stayed by her to the end, and at that end her stern mother-in-law at last softened.

"As you know, Grace," she said, "I always opposed Jim's marriage. But it's you who has been the real daughter to me, and not my own."

So after many years she died and was buried beside the husband whose failure she had despised. Then Grace went to put away her things which had come down from the years of affluence, her sealskin sacque, and her long Paisley shawl and her black silk shawl with the embroidery and jet beads, and the brooches and the heavy silk dresses.

But when she opened her mother-in-law's trunk, it was empty. The daughters had made good use of their time. Short as their visit had been, it had been long enough to divide between them and to carry secretly away all that was left of value to the mother whom they had ignored for twenty years.

Chapter 10

SOME PEOPLE say that it was a Forty-niner who had made his fortune and was on his way home to one of the back-country towns up the river. He had come as far as the Mills and must have arrived in the afternoon. But he had struck it rich in California. He sported a big gold chain and a fine open-faced watch which he looked at often. He let it be known that his family would be surprised at what he carried in the bag in his hand. Excitement had made him talkative. Excitement made him unwilling to stay at the Mills till morning, as a sensible man would have done. No, he must start for home, immediately, on foot. He didn't mind walking.

But night overtook him in sparsely settled country where the poor woods farms are scattered at long intervals along a rutted road, and at one of these he must have stopped and ask for lodging for the night. Nothing more is known of him, except that he never reached home and there is a story of a schoolteacher who for years opened school and conducted classes with the aid of a great gold watch which lay on her desk and which none of the pupils ever dared to touch, though often enough they wondered what initials, if any, were cut into the case whose back they never saw.

But this is not the usual story they tell of the haunting of Morton's woods, the long stretch of green which lies between Taniscot Pond and the river on the unfrequented Back Road. In the days when people drove in buggies, young couples were always warned to see to it that they were through the woods well before dusk, and surely with good reason if the tales of what some have beheld there are true.

Some say that the Morton house is still standing, unoccupied when we last passed that way, at the beginning of the woods. But others say that it stood where there is only a cellar hole in a bit of overgrown meadow by a stream, the one opening in the very midst of the woodlands as you drive along.

This is a story of the Yankee peddler, that romantic and often tragic figure in our nineteenth century, about whom legends cling in every part of the East. He came from the unknown and passed into the unknown, bringing with him the gossip of the whole countryside, messages from up the road, and a cart filled with enticement for man, woman, and child. He was usually a being of great force of personality, of wit and persuasiveness, a teller of tall tales, a liar with his tongue in his cheek, and he must also have had courage, for he stopped at very out-of-the-way doors and had with him not only a cart filled with merchandise but a wallet filled with money as well.

All that is known of the peddler of Morton's woods is that he stopped at old man Morton's and never went on again. But there was no proof of foul play, and no one to demand justice for a stranger. Still there was talk. The occasional neighbor, stopping to chat, found Morton's poor kitchen spruce with new tin pans, and a fresh broom always behind the door. The womenfolk too had new calico dresses and the two big sullen Morton boys had new axes when they went chopping in the interminable woods that stretched about their fences. Some people went so far as to claim that they recognized the horse which did their plowing and hauling, and had last seen it between the shafts of a peddler's cart. But though the talk went on as country talk will, no one did anything about it, or probably ever would have.

However, as the months went on and the years, a change took place in old man Morton. He'd been breaking up fast, as everyone noticed, and he seemed uneasy all the time as though his conscience wasn't sitting well inside him. He began to drop hints of dark things on his mind, and people noticed one or other of his boys always kept in earshot to give old man Morton a black look and shut him up when he began to talk that way. But the old man took less and less heed of them and their looks. His business appeared to be with his Maker.

Then one day the neighbors heard that old man Morton was dead. His family buried him without asking anyone in to see him. They said he'd died of a stroke.

The countryside thought that over for a while. "Stroke," they began to say when they'd thought enough. "Like as not it was a stroke of an ax in the back of the head. Those boys of his was real anxious about what old man Morton was going to say next." And again no one did anything about it, for it was after all strictly a family affair.

But if you were to take the old Back Road after dusk you might to this day see a terrible thing. Out of the bushes an old man with a flying white beard would burst, and go running stiff-legged across the road, his coattails flapping awkwardly behind him. And almost before you had had time to see the ax buried half to the hilt in his white head, another figure would jump out of the woods and take off after him, with *his* coattails flapping, and an ax in *his* head too. The second man would be younger altogether and go racing after the first in long revengeful bounds, so that you would say that he must come up with him any minute; but terror would somehow keep the old man just out of reach, and for as long as you dared listen you would hear the two crashings move farther and farther off through the dense woods, on the other side of the road.

Which explains why no one chooses that route after dark even with a car, unless he has plenty of gasoline, good tires, and headlights he can trust.

Chapter 11

Two years ago our telephone on the farmers' line was still working, and Tom was not in uniform. He was just finishing his supper with Grace in the big kitchen when the repeated five rings from the pantry announced that some one was calling us. Grace answered. It was Mrs. Hardy. There'd been some trouble that evening in getting in the cows, and one had stayed out somewhere in the wild pasture. Because her legs were better than Walter's, Mrs. Hardy had gone after the creature; but by the time she'd got the strayed cow started for the barn Walter was gone, and he didn't answer when she called. He must be off in the woods.

We all took a hurried look outside where the cold September night, gray with fog, was beginning to close in. Tom slipped into his sweater.

"I'll pick up that man down at the cottage," he said, and was gone.

Grace telephoned Alicia Hill at the head of the road. She knew everyone and would spread the alarm. Henry and I got into our car and drove past Mrs. Hardy, who waved her stick in greeting from the shed door, and so on to the two Sherman houses half a mile farther down the road. Neither of them had a telephone. We picked up Gene the postmaster. Norman at the other house wasn't in, but his family said they'd send him right along. We drove back, bumping along the narrow road between the Hardys' hayfields and the Heath, left the car, and started for the upper pasture.

"You follow the path down towards the Cove," said Gene as we climbed over the bars. "I'll look in the beech woods."

I shall never forget the way in which he melted away into the woods to our left, moving very fast with less air of effort than I have ever seen used. Henry and I started down the crude cart track which led through young pines, boulders, and snatches of grass into the pine and beech forest beyond. The first stars were beginning to show here and there where there was less fog, and we knew that we must be quick. We had flashlights in our pockets, but Mr. Hardy must be found soon. He was too old a man to stand the exposure of a cold Maine night for long, and already it was late September.

We had not gone far, however, when we saw something coming towards us through the gloom. It was Tom and another man, a stranger; and between them they carried, on a seat made of their four hands clasped at the wrists, the heavy weight of Mr. Hardy, his great head between theirs and his stick still held in one big hand flung over Tom's shoulder. Henry and I hurried back for the car and drove it across the hayfield to the bars, where the young men lifted Mr. Hardy into the front seat. As we drove slowly back across the field we met Raymond Bremen and his hired man.

Mr. Hardy growled, "What the devil are you doing here, Raymond?"

In another moment it was John Stahl.

"What the devil you doing here, John?"

The farmyard was filled with old trucks and cars. Not a farm on our road but had sent its man to help find Mr. Hardy. In the wide dark doorway of the shed Mrs. Hardy stood, the cow staff still in her hand.

"What did you think you were doing, Hardy?" she asked mildly, only the "Hardy" showing that she was upset, for on usual occasions she calls him Walter. The young men carried him into the kitchen and set him in his big rocking chair with the cushion by the stove. They had found him nearly a mile away in the woods. His legs had given out, and he was dragging himself home by his strong arms, trailing his body behind him. He had gone through a barbed-wire fence and across a brook, but he was still full of fight. For some time he wouldn't sit on their linked hands but tried to walk, and they were nearly exhausted in carrying his weight, upright, between them up the hill. His first question was for Mrs. Hardy.

"Addie all right?"

"I thought Addie was lost," he explained.

That evening Grace went down with Henry's flask of brandy to help Mrs. Hardy make Mr. Hardy comfortable. The trucks and the cars were gone. The old people were alone in the kitchen, but Mr. Hardy would not go to bed. He sat in the big chair, wrapped in blankets, drinking his brandy and hot water, his eyes fixed reflectively on nothingness.

"Man and boy," Grace heard him say, almost to himself, "man and boy, I had them all with me."

[39]

Chapter 12

THE YOUNG PEOPLE whom I found in our parlor were strangers to me. They were hot, excited, and here and there flecked with clay. It was a little while before I understood what had happened. It seems that they were camping at the foot of Roger Hill's field on the point, and that somehow they had discovered an old spring among our alders. They had asked Mr. Maurice Hill if there had ever been a spring there and he said yes. It was what our farm had mostly used for drinking. It was all filled in with mud, but as they dug down they came on the remnants of barrel staves; and when at last they had cleared out the loose clay the sides had seemed firm, and the water began to come in clear.

"The first New England spring I ever drank from was in the woods on Pond Island off Cherryfield," I said. "It flowed into a barrel and there was a cocoanut shell to drink from."

The young people looked at each other and smiled.

"Do you know the wonderful thing about this? About a foot and a half down in the mud we found a cocoanut shell! If you'll come down to our camp tomorrow for tea we'll give it to you. It isn't even cracked."

I knew whose spring it was. It was Captain Dan'l's spring. The lost spring. Mrs. Hardy had spoken of it often

—down somewhere near the end of the wall in the alder thicket; but we had never found it. Captain Dan'l was the first sole owner of this farm. In 1830 he, as younger son, had been given this slice of the point as his share. The outlines of his first log cabin can still be seen above our house after the hay has been cut. We know a lot about him, for he was an old man when Mrs. Hardy was a child just down the lane.

" 'Pumpkin on two sticks,' we children used to call him," she will say, chuckling at the memory. "He was a little man with thin legs and a fat stomach. You know, he was a shoemaker. His shop used to stand over by the barn."

Yes, we knew the shop; but we had torn it down, for it had been too long a chicken house in later years for us to find a use for it. But we have his round cobbler's stone still to hold open our side door.

"He didn't like children," Mrs. Hardy used to tell us. "He'd chase us away, but we'd come back. No, I don't know why he was called Captain. His wife was Nabby. Once the trapdoor in the kitchen was open for something, and he came in suddenly and fell straight down into the cellar. I can still hear him swear. I remember he went out on the ice once in a cutter on a Sunday, and the horse broke through and was drowned. People said it happened because it was Sunday. It didn't keep Captain Dan'l from taking horses out on the ice though. Another time he had Nabby with him on the lake and the horse ran away.

" 'That horse just went up at both ends; but I held tight to Nabby and Nabby held tight to the sleigh, and we came out all right,' was the way he told it. You know your farm was what we call a dry farm. Besides the lake there was only that marshy well back of the barn and that little bricked-in spring halfway down the field, and then the spring that's been lost. That was the only water Captain Dan'l would drink. Many a time I've gone with one of his grandchildren taking a pail to get Captain Dan'l fresh water from that spring. And when he lay dying that was the water he asked for. They were all so upset and busy that someone got him water from the near spring instead, thinking he'd never notice the difference, close to his end as he was. But he did. Sat right up in bed. 'That water never came from my spring,' he said. And he wasn't satisfied till they brought him the right water. It was the last he ever drank."

Since then a big spring flowing from rock has been blasted out near the house and covered with a spring-house; but here on a farm which is loved every bit of tradition is dear to us, and I had often wondered about Captain Dan'l's spring. And now it was the gift of these two eager young strangers.

We went down to see them late the next afternoon, taking our two little girls with us, past the historic slope where Margaret when five, and alone picking wild strawberries, had met the terrifying old woodchuck, over the woodchuck's wall, and into the Hill fields. The hay had not yet been cut and was still trembling and running with every stray breeze; but a broad path led straight to the bank of alders that ringed the pond. In a hollow stood the encampment, more like Isopel Berners' camp in the dingle than anything I have ever seen in America. A tent stood on one side, a light trailer on the other, and a fire burned in a ring of stones opposite. A rod between two near-by alder bushes had been fitted with hooks from which clean saucepans and frying pans were hanging. Three stone steps just beyond led down to the water, where a canoe and a little sailing boat were moored. A cat and a large kitten came to meet us, their tails held straight and high in friendly greeting, and while the children roasted marshmallows and the kettle began to boil we were shown about.

The tent was floored and carpeted. A wide bed with a white coverlet filled most of the space, but there was room for a small bureau and a writing table and chair by the opening. A pair of steps led into the covered trailer where stood the small icebox and an old chest of drawers painted white and used as a kitchen cabinet. Several wicker chairs stood about on the grass by the fire and, with the cats, completed the sense of an actual home which happened to have the sky for a roof and the pond for a front dooryard.

"We've learned to camp comfortably," they explained to us. "You see we are both ministers. We met at the theological school and began to preach soon after we were married, though I [here it was the wife speaking] don't preach often, but try to run the Sunday school and take what work I can from my husband's shoulders. Every year we have a two weeks' vacation. Hotels and camps are so expensive, but someone is always willing to let us use their land, and we like it better this way."

They left a few days later. Only a square of mowed green and three stone steps between the alders showed where they had been. By the time we managed to get a barrel for Captain Dan'l's spring it was too late in the year to put it in and now Tom is in the army and Captain Dan'l's spring is filling in with clay again. But we have the cocoanut shell without a crack in it, and we know where the lost spring is; and some day, sooner or later, the clay will be cleaned out again, and the water used, if only by the haymakers in the lower field. And I hope Captain Dan'l and his Nabby up in the graveyard between the two maples will feel pleased.

Chapter 13

Fɪʀᴇ! Nᴏ ᴏɴᴇ in the cities can have an idea of what that word means to a farmer in such country as ours. If a building catches fire it is as good as lost. Often enough there is no telephone; if there is one, by the time the little fire apparatus from the next town has reached the spot the roof is already burning up from the cellar hole under the shriveling elms which share the fate of the house. The summer lightning storms here are serious things, and people like the Hardys get up and dress at night when they hear that heavy rumble and see the flick of lightning down the sky, to let out the stock if the barn should catch. In cities I never seem to take lightning very seriously; but three trees near us have been struck and split in half since we came here, and the fine Bremen barn at the head of our lake replaces one which was burned down, as Mrs. Bremen has told us:

"The men were hurrying to get in the very last load of hay. There was a cloud overhead no bigger than your hand,

and out of it came a crack and a flare which struck the barn; and it was burned down, and in it all the hay for the stock for the next year."

Last week a heifer at Roundtop Farms was struck and killed. Oh, we respect lightning around here! It has a way of snapping on a lavender light in the middle of our rooms, and of cracking down our hallways like a whip. But lightning is not the danger that stoves and chimneys are. Two houses on our short road have been burned to the ground and under the ground since we have lived here. The second was an old low house of one story which belonged to the young Shermans. They had made it look very nice, with fresh paint at the sills, and flowers by the door. The young husband was away from home, working at the shipyard. The young wife had gone into the garden patch to weed, leaving something cooking on the oil stove. The two-year-old girl was taking her nap in the bedroom just beyond the kitchen.

Well, Mrs. Sherman never could tell what she heard or saw or smelled. Her back was to the little house, but suddenly she whirled, dropped her hoe, and ran for the blazing kitchen. She burned off her eyebrows and lashes getting into the bedroom, but she dropped the child safely out of the window and followed her down. A road gang was at work on Route No. 1 not more than a hundred yards away, and there were three men at the store across a narrow field. But not a single thing was saved except a newly painted screen which had been left leaning against the side of the house.

"What do I care for the place if they're all right?" said young Mr. Sherman when he heard the news at the shipyard.

But last month Taniscot itself nearly burned down. It was by merest chance that we were taking our once-a-week trip the nine miles to town. About two or three miles away we became aware of great billows of smoke darkening the horizon beyond us. Having been fooled before, we said easily, "Probably someone's burning wet hay across the river." But as we curved up the last hill we saw that the town was burning. A house on the Pocassett Road was quietly flaming like a well lighted grate. Although a brisk wind was blowing I only remember high red flames rising straight and orderly into the air. Half a mile away in the heart of town the smoke was rising in great twisting puffs from several places at once. A little fire engine from the largest neighboring village passed us with a wail of sirens. It had come thirty miles. As we stopped and backed our car into a drive I leaned out and asked a woman what had happened. She was wearing a flowered apron and was busy tying a pail of water to a cord whose other end was held by a man braced upright on the slope of the shingle roof above her.

"Taniscot's burning down," she said, not loudly, but like a cry.

As we stood there benumbed, a white silky fluff of smoke began to stream from the church steeple which stands so nobly at the upper end of the town, its steps and Greek columns looking down the length of the village street. A sort of shudder of despair seized the crowd when they knew that the church had caught. Everywhere there were firemen from eight different towns, and the soldiers, who had been quartered in the hotel, were busy dumping truck-loads of cots and uniforms and equipment here and there in different parts of the village. I saw even boxes of eggs from the military kitchen spilled unbroken on the grass, and on the back streets where I walked while Henry went over to help friends wet down their roof, I found people gathered in wedges, watching the beloved steeple between the shoulders of the intervening houses. Somehow they had got a hose onto the steep ridgepole. Men in fire helmets were outlined against the sky, bound together by the heavy swag of the fire hose. The bell struck once for half-past one, and someone said, "We may never hear that again"; but a few minutes later it rang out suddenly three times as though in alarum. By that time men had reached the steeple itself and were hacking away at the burning latticework. The smoke was coming less thickly. In fact, in the center of town too the smoke was dying down. As I turned into the main street the river showed with unusual brightness and breadth, for Mrs. Hill's white boarding house was half burned away, and the old brick building of the *County News* was nearly down to the ground. Behind it a smoking ugly gap showed where the Military Garage had stood over the water. The little white house next to it and the white house opposite were blackened cellar holes, and men were still fighting fire on the wide roofs of the old hotel where the soldiers had been billeted for months.

But in every store the clerks were at their counters, and I met a woman walking away from one with her arms filled with knobby packages.

"How did it start?" I asked someone. I have no idea now who it was, but I remember her answer very well:

"It was the sun," she said, "on some bottles in a dump below the garage. One of them formed a burning-glass and set fire to some rags near by. There were some boys who saw it and could have stopped it easily, but they let it go too long."

There have been other explanations since, though none so likely nor so circumstantial as hers. But in whatever way the fire started no one has any doubt as to why it was stopped.

"If it hadn't been high tide the whole town would have gone. But, being high tide, they could get enough water for the hoses. There were two pumping right here at the slope and six more down on the wharf. All the towns sent their engines."

So the sun set the fire and the river put it out, and Taniscot is managing in the way in which Maine people always manage. Somehow the *County News* has installed itself in a little unused grocery in time to record its own destruction, and the soldiers are camping at the fair grounds, and the community has made room for the families who have lost their homes, and the church, with one side of its steeple blackened and charred, and gray water stains marring the white of its columns, defiantly celebrated its hundredth birthday with a fair and a supper, the very next week.

Chapter 14

It was on a day early in May that we came to the Ark. Henry insisted that we should reach it for the first time by water; so we drove to the Mills with our supplies for ten days piled in the Taggetts' car, and there hired a fishing boat with an outboard motor and its elderly "captain" accustomed to taking fishermen down the pond in a search for landlocked salmon—or black bass, failing salmon.

As we chugged slowly along the tentacle of water which curls off from the main lake for four or five miles to the Mills, I watched the hilly shores on either side with their variegated pattern of farmland and woods, and the narrow islands which at a distance have the look of schooners in an anchorage. As we swung into the wider reaches of the main lake with the Persia Hills in the distance, my enthusiasm grew. A loon watched us—a great brightly colored bird, curious and attentive. When it had seen enough it dived from sight, reappearing a long time afterwards, much farther away. I had not yet heard the wild ululation of its call to which I was so often to listen in the darkness of a night before rain, but already I was vaguely aware that here was one of the guardians of these waters.

We had turned now into a green bay between woods. Two islands lay at its entrance, and beyond to the right was a glimpse of beach; but our eyes were fixed mostly on the slopes to the left, which in two places showed the long scars of recent cutting over. The slashes were, however, relieved by stretches of untouched pines and hemlocks crowding close to the water's edge.

"That's part of the farm," Henry said, keeping the excitement out of his voice.

Now the bay turned at right angles like the foot of a Christmas stocking. Gone were the distant islands and the more distant blue hills. Here only unstirred water lay in a deep fold of forested slopes—for these trees were not woodland trees but forest trees, many of them first-growth pines reaching up and up towards that incomparable sheer wall of cliff which we were later to call the Chinese Wall.

Not a house, not a trail, not a sign of man nor his work touched the purity of the scene, except that in the center of the pine-reflecting water lay a boat, such as a child might dream of. It was shaped like a toy Noah's Ark, with a narrow deck along its sides that widened at the bow. Low, many-paned windows with curtains drawn back lined most of the walls; but the roof, instead of being peaked, was flat, and a convenient ladder led up to it—a place for diving for those who liked diving, and for stargazing for those who might prefer stargazing.

As we thundered into Green Cove, filling all the hollow places with the racket of our engine, we must have guessed that it was a place of echoes, where later we should hear the call of a thrush returned, and our own shouts tossed back to us in a cascade of cries, each one fainter and farther off than its fellow. A place of echoes and of reflections. I shall never forget the Ark in that early May. No one was there, but Henry climbed aboard and opened the door with a key he had in his pocket. The old captain

[51]

helped us to unload the bags and baskets of supplies. Then he brought us the rowboat which was moored to a solitary landing with a lantern on a pole beside it, and so left us to our borrowed kingdom.

At that time the Ark was, I think, only a year old. It had been built at the Mills, and the Taggetts' idea was that they would have it towed to different parts of the lake and spend a few weeks or months, now in this cove and now in that. But once they had taken possession of Green Cove they were never able to move on. For one thing they never wanted to, and for another they lost the anchor next year, so that they were forced to moor alongshore; and later still leaks began to appear and the Ark had to remain in what had been its original winter quarters at the head of the cove, where the stream had spread a little meadow for the Hardys' cows and the deer and occasional moose.

But when we landed on the Ark that May, lost anchors and leaks in the scowlike underhull were things far off in the impenetrable future. The vessel rode its mirror of water serenely. Eagerly as children we went past the green icebox and down the three or four steps into the interior.

I suppose no woman ever grows too old to love a doll's house; and I have heard wives declare that their husbands' passion for sailing-boats was more than half due to the fun the men had keeping house in a little cabin. The Ark had all the doll's-house quality, but it was large enough so that one did not feel cramped in it on a rainy day. We entered a single long room with windows on either side and two doors and a bookcase along its back. A neat beguiling sink to our right was overhung by dish shelves. Then came a wood stove, a huge copper kettle filled with dry wood beside it, and a table folding down below the windows with four canvas-seated chairs drawn up to it. Under the bookcase there was another table, with a jug of lilacs and magazines; and a couch stood under the windows to the left, with a small jog beyond for the toilet-room, on whose outer wall hung raincoats and fishing hats. The two doors flanking the bookcase led into two cabins—each with a large window, a double lower berth, a single upper berth that had its own small high window, and a rounded shelf and mirror in the remaining corner.

Such was and is the working plan of the Ark; but to know its quality one should know the details, the orderliness with which all the cooking things are fitted into their places, the charm of the hooks made from hard peeled crotches of wood, the pattern of the Hindu cotton on the couch, the amusing wooden birds and animals along the bookcase shelf which come from Andy's own workroom in the shed of the old house in Taniscot where he rests himself when tired with painting and illustrating. It had taken the combined practical sense and poetry of Andy and Sue to create the Ark.

I forget some of the details of our lives for the next ten days. I think that the Taggetts once came from town to see us and brought us fresh supplies. Was it every day or every other day that we rowed to the wharf, moored our boat, and walked through the thrush-haunted woods into the Hardys' pasture—which was then misted over with the lovely little flower called bluet or quaker-ladies—and so, keeping carefully to the path so as not to spoil the young hay, reached the Hardys' house for half an hour's talk in the kitchen, fresh milk in a pail, fresh eggs in a basket, and two glass cider jugs filled with well water? We carried the jugs on leather straps easier for the hand than any handle, and I remember that Henry was proud of me on the evening when I guided our expedition safely back to the waiting rowboat through the darkness along a thread of trail. We had not been married quite two years at the time, and I was still making excuses to say "my husband." It sounded so pleasant—and still does. "We" is a much wider-open door than "I." You see a good deal more of life from it, a brighter landscape, a wider view. Henry is particularly good at widening a wife's view because he knows everything—knows the names of constellations even when they appear upside down in their inconsequential way, knows the names of birds and of all historical characters, knows books and living people and why they do what they do. This is wonderfully arousing in certain aspects, and convenient in others for a woman with a short memory; but it's particularly nice to have so much scholarship stored away in a person full of warmth and wit. You feel Henry the moment he comes into a room; and it's not just because he's big and good-looking, though that helps, but because he is charged to an extraordinary degree with life and a kind of compassionate humanity. All the same, he hasn't a strong sense of direction in the woods, and his favorite cry in strange hotels is "Lead, kindly wife." If he will never make a Maine guide, he has a Napoleonic quickness and sureness of decision. He had been at Taniscot visiting the Taggetts the month before, and on his way back from a weekend at the Ark had heard Andy accosted by an old farmer who was walking past their car, stuck deep at the moment in the ruts of mud time:

"Know anyone who'd like to buy my farm, Mr. Taggett?"

"No, I don't, Mr. Beals."

"It's next to the Hardys on Hill's Neck," Andy explained later to Henry.

And Henry thought, "*I'd* like to buy it."

He told me about it while we were having a fish luncheon at a Quincy restaurant. He drew rough plans of Hill's Neck and Green Cove on a menu. He had never set foot on the land, but he liked the district, the feel of the lake and countryside. He had no need to go shopping, to look at this town house or that cottage on a salt river, to weigh the hills of Vermont against the elms of Connecticut.

Casually, carelessly, but surely, he chose the place he wanted for a home. He had only seen the farmhouse at a distance so much in need of paint and so disfigured by added accretions of plank verandas that he had thought it would have to be torn down. He drew dreadful pictures of it on the menu, which the house today would not care to see.

So that was why we were on the Ark, cooking our meals, sweeping our doll's house, swimming on the warm afternoons, walking through the woods to the Hardys.

It was not until the third day that Henry rowed me over to a very small beach against a wall of pine boughs which swung open to the beginnings of a path. "Betsy's Landing," he named it as I stepped ashore, for the first time setting foot on what was to be, by the end of another week, our land.

Chapter 15

THERE IS one daughter in the Kimball family and ten sons. They come of mixed Yankee and Knoxboro Dutch stock, and the young children of the family have skins of such rose-leaf pinkness and such milky whiteness that they might be little princes and princesses.

The boys have worked out as farm hands until they have saved enough money to marry and settle down on their own farms. We have been fortunate enough to have two of the younger sons with us, Grainger, who has recently won the silver star in North Africa, and for the last two years Tom now part of a gun crew at the Boston Airfield. They are brown-faced, strong-backed, pleasant-looking boys, but the handsomest of the family is Phil with his shock of yellow hair, his bright blue eyes, and his quick smile.

Phil is a raiser of oxen. He always has at least two yoke, and now he has a tiny pair of calves which he is breaking in for his little boy. Ever since we came to the farm, Phil has plowed our garden, and I have memories of watching through flowering apple branches the deliberate motion of the oxen, the slow rolling-back of the earth from the plow, and Phil behind them with one foot in the furrow and the other trampling the sods down into place while Grainger walked hieratically beside the beasts motioning with his goad. I have happened upon Phil against a sky line working two yoke together at the plow, forcing the heavy autumn earth. And at the fair the children and I have applauded him at the drag where he usually competes and wins in the middleweight class.

The oxen we knew best were Star and Lion, an unmatched team, rather thin, and with none of the Roman beauty that some of the greater oxen display. Star was black and white, Lion a brindled yellow. Year after year Phil threatened to sell them.

"They're getting old," he'd say. "I could sell them as working oxen, but they might get where they wouldn't be fed proper, and they've been too good workers for me to want that to happen. No, I'll have them butchered this fall."

But the next spring when we heard the heavy rumble of the cart which held plow and harrow coming along the lane, we would all run out, and the children would shout with relief and joy:

"It's Star and Lion again! It's Star and Lion!"

We knew them so well—which one ate salt and which one didn't, which one liked to go swimming and which one didn't, which one lay down to rest and which one remained standing. Catherine learned to feed them and drive them, to know on which shoulder to tap an ox when she wanted him to turn, what to yell when they were to stand still or back up, even how the great blue yoke was put on and taken off. Last year at ten she was a competent ox driver. When the plowing was finished that June, we all got into bathing suits and Phil drove Star and Lion yoked into the pond. They waded slowly out, deeper and deeper into the water, obedient still. Now the water was up to their shoulders, now it covered their backs, now they were obediently swimming, necks outstretched, eyes rolling a little. Phil swam beside them with the children swimming too. They made a great curve, startling the loons, and then waded ashore to browse on young leaves, up to their knees in water.

But next spring another pair, far prettier than Star and Lion, came with Phil. They were sturdy, well matched, and clearly colored in red and white. Their names were Broad and Bright, and they stayed at the farm a whole week, hauling logs and taking the blue cart down into the woods to clear brush. Henry and the pug and I rode in the cart, seated on some hay, along the wood roads, and nearly had the teeth jolted out of our heads. But we have rarely enjoyed ourselves more, and never have I been so impressed as by the beautiful precision with which the slow, loosely harnessed animals manipulated that wagon down wood roads just wide enough to clear the axles. We had lunch on a rock over Green Cove, while the oxen slowly ate their grass among the pines. They were so bright in their coloring that the shadowy pine woods didn't darken them. They looked like the charming toys old farmers whittle out on winter evenings. But they were not like old Star and Lion to us. We didn't know their habits. They didn't go swimming with their master.

This spring Phil was using still another pair. He had sold Broad and Bright to an old man who wanted them for hauling logs out of his wood lot last winter. Somehow one afternoon the old man slipped and fell between the an-

[58]

imals and the slowly moving and heavily loaded sled. He yelled to them to whoa as he felt himself going; and without moving one step further they both stopped.

"If those two steers hadn't been so well trained, I'd not be here today," he told Phil. "I'll never butcher them. They can live out their lives and die of old age."

There is a strong feeling here between the drivers and their oxen, although it is never forgotten that when a horse is old he is no good for anything, but that an old ox still makes good beef. The Maine farmers are realistic, yet many an ox dies in pasture. I remember once having tea under the big locust tree at the Hills' next door. Among the guests there was a young couple, who had traveled much abroad and knew the great cities of the world, but had roots in this countryside.

The talk happened to turn to oxen.

"I always remember a wonderful pair my father had," the wife said. "They would do anything he told them. He didn't have to shout at them even. He had a cord, not much more than a string, attached to one of their horns, and he could lead them anywhere by that, without using the goad at all. He was very proud of them, of course. Then the last war came along and they were offering high prices for beef to send overseas. There was a mortgage on the farm which worried Father, and the price he could get for the oxen would just pay off the mortgage. He talked it over with Mother and made up his mind to sell them. He took them down to where they were loading a livestock freight car. A lot of other men had brought their oxen too. They had to go up an incline of boards—like a gangplank, you know—into the car, and the men were having a terrible time getting their oxen up it. They seemed to know something was wrong. But Dad's oxen trusted him, so they followed him right up as though they were just going into the barn. And that always troubled him as long as he lived, the way his oxen had followed him that day."

Chapter 16

THERE WAS a woman who lived in Taniscot about the middle of the last century when it was a center of shipping and exported the oak and pine of its woods, the ice of its lakes, and the red brick made in the yards along its river banks to most of the world. She kept a sailors' boarding house, ostensibly, but she had a good trade on the side in selling winds.

Although one thinks of a witch, particularly a seaport witch, as a rather cosmopolitan person, this woman seems to have retained a good deal of local pride. So one evening when she heard two captains in her boarding house boasting of their respective vessels, which were waiting ready-laden for Boston, and of their general handiness and remarkable speed, she naturally took the side of the Taniscot captain—the other was an outsider from Bath maybe, or maybe Bangor. Anyway the woman made some excuse to call the Taniscot captain out of the room, where he sat arguing with the other man.

When she had him in the darkness of the hall, she whispered to him fiercely:

"Bet him all you have, and I'll give and I'll give and I'll give you a wind, and you'll be in Boston by morning."

That sounded pretty impossible even to the Taniscot captain, but when a witch told you to do something in those days you did it, and asked no questions. So he went back and laid the bet with the other man and then roused up his crew and went down to his vessel and hauled up anchor in the dark—or what dark there was, for the moon was rising. There was a downriver wind rising too, of which there'd been no hint earlier in the evening, so they made good time with an outgoing tide. When they sailed into the ocean a strange thing happened: the following wind veered into the east—it was still a following wind. There was no tacking, no feeling about to keep the sheets filled, nothing at all for the captain and crew to do but set all sail and dance down the coast while the cook put the coffee to boil on the galley stove. Hour after hour went by, and the wind never faltered nor shifted again. Like a big broom sweeping a ball of paper before it, that breeze carried the Taniscot vessel straight to the entrance of Boston Harbor and then, with a sidewise flick, it tossed her in.

The moon was gone and the morning star was just beginning to pale and there was light on the eastern horizon when the ship came in to its usual berth at T Wharf after such a voyage as no Maine vessel ever has had before or since.

"Got in kind of early, didn't you, Captain?" asked the watchman, holding his lantern for the captain to step ashore.

The captain nodded.

"Had a fair wind," he said laconically.

Chapter 17

I SAT LOOKING from time to time at the portrait of a woman opposite the marble fireplace. The room was filled with flowers and people in evening dress, and the talk about me was good; but no face in the room had as much character as the long face of the portrait, and no talk took my imagination as did the stories I knew about her.

It was a cold evening, and the parlor shades were down and the curtains were drawn against the autumn darkness outside. There was of course a fire burning on the hearth. I knew that we were nearly half a mile away from the nearest house, and that far below us, beyond old hayfields and orchards gone back to woodland, the river flowed dark and cold down to the sea.

The woman in the portrait with the quiet resolved face had been mistress of this house in her time. She had sat before this Italian mantel drinking her cup of tea, perhaps wearing the same dark dress and white lace collar fastened with a cameo brooch in which the artist had painted her.

She was as intrinsically American as the house, whose granite sills had been quarried from the rock of its own pastures, whose woodwork had been made from the trees of its own woodlands, and whose bricks had been baked from its own soil. I had seen the mold for the bricks still preserved in the cellar storerooms. She too had been born of this land; but there was little in her face to tell what a strange role she had been given to play.

For she had been a sea captain's wife, and had gone to sea with her husband. I judge that he traded largely with the West Indies and perhaps with Charleston and New Orleans. Fever and plague and smallpox were as much a part of the chances of that life as were hurricanes or the doldrums. She risked them all with her captain: during a mutiny she sat on the money box with a pistol in each hand, but in a more terrible and long drawn-out ordeal she navigated the ship with the aid of only a cabin boy, while her husband lay on the deck sick with yellow fever and when not delirious gave her what directions he could. The rest of the crew were either dead or sick below decks. She and the young boy set the course and steered, reefed and unreefed the sails, nursed the sick and fed them, until finally their signal of distress was picked up and help was sent them from a passing ship.

But the captain recovered to sail again, and quietly she packed her boxes and closed her big red house over its garden so that she might sail with him.

On this last voyage it was she who came down with yellow fever, and it was the captain who nursed her. Before she died she begged him to take her home and bury her in the graveyard above the river. It was against the law to bring ashore anyone who had died of a contagion, but he promised it should be done; and we may hope she died the easier for that promise.

Was it weeks or months later that the light sleepers of the town were wakened by a team of horses driving before dawn along the road from the city with a hogshead in the wagon behind them? Two men were in the cart, and some people recognized the captain and his brother; but getting ahead of the revenue officers with a clandestine unloading of liquor was no new thing on the Maine coast, and everyone wished the early passers-by well of their errand. Just what that errand really was, however, they had not yet suspected, though later people living near the graveyard spoke of mysterious sounds of spades on stones and of movings and stirrings in the darkness.

And to this day when the wind blows up from the river they say that it carries a smell of rum from the graveyard.

It is a small and beautiful burying ground with one enormous oak tree in it and a fine view over the river with the town of Taniscot rising from the other shore. The tide seems always to be flooding greenly in or out, and the sea gulls settle along the bank and the small land birds fly in and out of the rosebushes on the graves. Henry and I went there to hunt for the grave of the captain's wife. We had forgotten her name, and we read headstone after headstone, sometimes leaning down to part the grasses so that we might finish reading some verse engraved in a copybook hand.

Small as the graveyard was, however, it had been settled by an adventurous race, and among the many graves of the men who had followed the sea we found three tombstones to captains' wives who had died of fever or smallpox far from their homes on the Taniscot.

Chapter 18

In the days when David the little bull roamed in peace down the lanes of Monhegan Island and the sheep throve unchidden on the short sweet grass above the Heads, a fisherman was drowned, as many have been—thrown overboard by some accident and carried quickly under by the weight of his great sea boots. As often happens the spot was not far from shore; and when the wind died down his widow had herself rowed out in a dory to the place where he had been last seen alive. She had several things on the dory seat—his family Bible, for instance, and his old pair of carpet slippers, and his cat, tied up in a sack, and held on her lap.

When the dory reached the spot of ocean which represented her husband's grave, the woman threw in her offerings, as simply as a widow of the Stone Age might have attempted to bring ease and comfort to the spirit of the dead. Then she had herself rowed back again and took up her life as best she could.

Mrs. Laura E. Richards told us the story, which went back to her girlhood summers on Monhegan a little before or perhaps a little after the Civil War. Now the fishing is done from motorboats, which go much farther and faster than the old lobster smacks or dories, but the hard life is the same. Several years ago, on a fine day at Westport Island, a lobsterman took out his little boy for a summer afternoon of hauling pots along the coves and inlets. The motorboat was found later, empty, going with the tide down to the sea; in another twenty-four hours the man's body was found, but never the child's. People shook their heads and sighed. Perhaps the little boy had grown cramped in the boat and asked to get out on a rock—one of those long dark-sided backs of stone which rise up out of the water with a matted fur of seaweed ever stirring about them. Safe as the rock may have looked in the sunshine, it would be easy to slip on the wet surface. Although a man could not swim, and had on his lobsterman's boots, a father would have gone in after his little son, willy-nilly. But only the sea gulls would have seen what actually happened.

The life is hard and dangerous. Dangerous on a summer day, and more dangerous in winter. The lobster boats usually go out in pairs then, so that one may stand by the other in difficulties. Several winters ago two boats were hauling traps somewhere along the islands off Northeast Harbor. One of the men had some traps on a ledge above which the waves were apt to mount into high rollers, but without breaking.

On this particular day, while the other boat idled off the ledge, the first man went in to pull his traps. He had a boat hook in one hand—a long wooden staff ending in a gaff and hook—with which he was hauling a marker towards him, leaning well out over the gunwale while his boat tipped and tilted to the rollers.

Suddenly, against all expectation, a wave broke—broke over the boat and the leaning man, throwing him violently into the icy winter sea where his boots, after one floundering second, carried him feet-foremost straight down to the reef.

With incredible courage and coolness he held the boat hook straight up over his head. His chance to stand so on the reef, the tip of his boat hook visible in the hollow of the rollers, could last only a minute or two; and where one wave had broken, another might be expected to break, swamping another boat.

But his partner saw the gaff above the water, and in that split second ran his boat in beside it. Between breaker and breaker he got his grip on it while the man standing on the reef under the sea held on to the other end and was jerked and dragged back to safety and to life. Of all the lobstering stories I have heard on the coast, this seems to me the most remarkable, and the most creditable to the spirit of man.

Chapter 19

A LONG with the fairs and church suppers which begin in early September, the community can expect a certain number of auctions for social diversion. Auctions of course differ greatly—there are good auctions and bad ones; but I never went to one so bad that the people present didn't enjoy it. The perfect auction, however, should take place on a fine summer's day, not too hot and not too cold. It should begin in the morning, and someone should sell coffee and sandwiches and doughnuts in the shed about noon. It is desirable that the house should be set in an agreeable position with a view, and that there should be a lawn with chairs, benches, and rugs scattered about it, partly in the shade, facing the auctioneer, whose table should be set a little away from the kitchen door of the house.

The auctioneer is a very important factor in the success of an auction as a social entertainment. First of all, he must not sell things in order, and according to a printed list. Such cold formalism rarely takes place in our part of the country; but on the one or two occasions we have met with it, it has blighted the auction instantly. No, it must be possible to wander discreetly into the house to look at the pictures still on the walls or the china not yet taken off the pantry shelves. One must be able to look over the hooked rugs by the steps and at last insert this or that object into the hands of the auctioneer's assistant, with the certainty that it will soon be insinuated into the flow of sales. Sure then of not having to wait too long to bid on the object of one's own desire, one can enjoy the auctioneer's methods. He should of course have humor and some knowledge of what he is handling. I like him to be a man with a tradition, too, like the one who presented Henry with a Bible, saying, "There are two things, sir, which we never sell under the hammer—the Holy Bible and the American flag." A little jovial roguery is not out of place, either. The habit of saying, "Someone over there bid fifty cents, and there's fifty cents over there—that's a dollar! Who'll bid a dollar-ten?" is all very good auctioneering sport, if the auctioneer can get away with it.

Then the crowd should be mixed; some summer people —the men in slacks, perhaps, and the women with their knitting in bright knitting-bags—should be there, but the backbone of the group should be local, with a real interest in the plow and harrow over by the barn door, and an eye to the tinware.

Mrs. Sherman once told me about an auction she had been to. The house was very poor, she said. An old man had lived there for years alone, and everything was grimy with dirt. She'd wanted to bid on a picture of a sailing ship.

"It was real pretty, and it kind of took my eye, but Norman said, 'Mother, where would you put it?' and I didn't really know *where* I'd put it. So I didn't bid, and it went for fifty cents. The woman who got it took it out of its frame when she got home, to wash the glass, and she found twenty-five dollars in bills back of the picture. Twenty-five dollars! and I nearly bought it myself."

Mrs. Sherman laughs. She likes jokes, even jokes on herself. Life is full of practical jokes, and this was one played on her; but she wasn't the only one. She goes on with amusement.

"A lot of people found money, after they got home, in the things they'd bought. It seems that the old man was a miser, and no one ever guessed it. But the funny part was about his bed. After the auction was over no one knew yet about his being a miser, and they took out his mattress and a lot of the old quilts to burn them up back of the house. They were so dirty no one wanted them, of course.

"Well, the joke of it was, no sooner did the fire get well started than they found that the bedding was full of money. Bills went up into the air like burning leaves— dollar bills and five-dollar bills and ten-dollar bills—all of them burning. Of course the men tried to put out the fire. That mattress was just about stuffed with bills. But pshaw! they couldn't put it out. They had to just stand there and watch all that money go up into the air."

And Mrs. Sherman laughs again at the jokes Fate plays on people.

Chapter 20

IN EVERY PROPER New England neighborhood there is a family in which the members have not spoken to each other for years. Perhaps the emotional life here is a little thin and turns bitter in the cold winters. Stevenson tells of the same thing in Scotland. In these northern countries the human metal takes cold and heat slowly, and holds its temperature over a long period. Occasionally there may be murder—in Maine the ax murder is the characteristic form in households where the ax stands always ready by the wood block in the shed; but usually ill feeling assumes no more outward expression than that of silence.

In the last generation, there were two brothers on our road who quarreled over some apples as big boys. No one knows exactly what the apples had to do with it, but no doubt they served as well as anything else to draw down the slowly accumulated rancors and rubbings of youth. At any rate the boys stopped speaking to each other. As time went on they married and had families. One inherited the family farm, and the other went to live at the place next door. One had stock but no barn. The other had a barn but no stock. In some way arrangements were made so that the stock should be kept in the barn. A dozen times a week the two men must have passed close to each other, and renewed their satisfaction in not speaking. Undoubtedly it became a grim game, likely to go on until death entered in.

But here Fate intervened. When they were elderly men one of them was in an apple tree and the other was passing along the road.

The man in the road suddenly yelled:

"Look out! You're sawing off the limb you're sitting on!"

The warning was given, the silence was broken, and from that day on the brothers spoke to each other. An apple tree had healed the wound which an apple tree had made.

Chapter 21

Mrs. Hardy was born in the house where she now lives as an old woman. She knew the clump of lilacs and the single roses as a girl; she knew where the strawberries grew thickest, and where to take her basket for blueberries. Sometimes she tells us about her family. Her father must have been an interesting man—a reader, I judge, of Tom Paine, and a New Englander in something of the eighteenth century manner. He brought water lilies to put into the tiny pond by Witch Bridge and sowed his fields to barley and rye. He was fond of fox hunting. It was one of his hounds which was taken to Bath on the train, and which swam the wide Kennebec and arrived home across totally unknown country the next morning. He was not a churchgoer by any means, and Mrs. Hardy chuckles as she remembers an occasion when the minister came to dinner and her father had to listen unwillingly to a long grace. Later something occurred to set him off swearing, and the minister felt it his duty to rebuke him. But Mrs. Hardy's father looked the guest good-humoredly in the eye. "That's all right, parson. You stick to your prayers, and I'll stick to my cussing. Neither of us means a durned thing by it."

As an old man he sat more and more in the ell formed by the low house and the woodshed. That is a southwest corner with a long view over the lonely Heath, the stretch of land which reminds one of the Scotch moors. At its farther edge he could see the two Sherman farms and the Cullen farm with its row of elms along the ridge. The lake was hidden from sight behind the house, but he was an old man wanting sunlight. His greatest pleasure was to watch the martins.

On the farms here everyone loves the martins, partly because they are great flycatchers about the barns, but more for their pure beauty and swiftness. A pair of tree swallows will preempt a bird-house and allow no other birds of any kind to nest there, but the martins love a colony. Mrs. Hardy's father had built a martin house big enough for twenty couples and fastened it to the peak of the woodshed roof. There the martins nested year after year, a great flock of birds, and greater when the young birds learned to fly. The old man would sit for hours watching them darting and circling and calling above him.

Then one winter he died. In the spring at the usual time the first martins returned. They circled uneasily about the house for some hours, perching along the shed, twittering in the eaves. They seemed to be waiting for something which didn't happen, and after a while they flew away. The martin house stood empty that summer, and the next spring the same thing happened.

After several years, during which not a martin had returned, Mr. Hardy took the useless martin house down.

"No use having the old thing around," he said.

Chapter 22

Oᴜʀ ᴘᴏɴᴅ is supposed to be about fourteen miles long, from the old and now disused sawmill at the top of our bay to the stream which enters it at the village of Hamilton. It is a charming body of water. We aren't fishermen, so I cannot say much about its landlocked salmon, its black bass, or its pickerel. I know that sometimes the young alewives will pass in a dark line about a foot wide following along the shore like a ribbon trembling as it is pulled through the water. We have watched it for ten or fifteen minutes at a time before the last alewife passed, remembering the beauty and sadness of the alewife run up the Cascades at the Mills, while the eagles perch in the oaks along the shore, glutted with fish.

I say "sadness" because I know of nothing else which shows so clearly the almost insupportable effort which Nature demands of its children, and which they are able somehow to make. It takes an alewife about twenty-four hours to climb the stair of white water from pool to pool under the village willows. There are two branches of the stream. The fish which turn to the left towards the falls are doomed to be packed in no time in barrels of salt for the West Indies trade, or to be dried to a curious gold and strung on wands to be sold in our village groceries, or to be given to local widows according to the original charter.

But the fish which turn to the right will live, to reach their goal, the lake. I have stood on the little bridges which make this run so charming, and have looked down for as long as I could bear to do it, watching some especial alewife, marked perhaps by a scar of silver on its blue-black side, try again and again to make the four- or five-foot dash up to the next basin of circling water, thick with resting fish. Obviously they succeed, but after what failures! what exhaustions! Again and again my fish tries it, springs out of its wild shelter into the full white downrush of the stream, breasts it nobly with all the impetus of its effort, rises, rises one foot, two feet, perhaps three feet, the spirit driving on the body, and then is borne back, sideways, still struggling, to the basin it had hoped to leave. There it swims for a while worn out, but not for long. Again you see the silver scar flash forward, again the fallible flesh flings itself against the terrible strength of the water, again it is defeated. But the roe must be born—who knows why it must be in a lake, and not in a river or in the sea where the schools live? But such is not the decree. My fish, with its side already scraped against some jagged rock against which it has been flung, must not give up trying until it succeeds or dies. There it goes again. Almost that trim dark shape reached the next pool, but at the white lip it was torn down once more. By this time I can all but hear it scream.

After a while I suggest that we go up to the dam, at this time partly opened, and watch the successful alewives, which have only now to have their young and die in peace. Yes, they are there, one or two arriving at a time, breasting the last current, swimming slowly into the quiet lake water. They have to me a dazed air, as of creatures which have reached their goal by so hard a road that they have forgotten what they wanted. They swim slowly about, recovering, I suppose. Altogether, the run of alewives is a sight very wonderful and sad. I cannot help but be reminded of what human beings suffer within the very simple framework of life—to be born, to find one's mate, to bring to life, and to die.

But, after all, our pond itself is not sad to look at nor to think about. Its variegated woodlands and farmlands are beautiful. It has hills and the promise of mountains beyond. From my window here I see a little empty white farmhouse with two big arborvitae trees beside it, and sitting underneath those trees with a picnic basket I have often looked up from unwrapping a covered dish of hot macaroni and cheese to see Mount Washington on the horizon. The swallows high above me at this moment can get an excellent view of the Camdens, going down in blue heights to the sea. So, although we actually see nothing higher than the Persia Hills from the lake, we know that we are but one remove from larger fry.

Our pond is prettily diversified by islands, coves, clean shores of stone and pine, and beguiling stretches of sheltered waters where the water lilies float, or the rushes rub against the sides of the canoe and the duck rise with a whistling of wings from their feeding. Below our own fields, we have seen moose tracks on the softened ice of the pond in March, but I have yet to meet with some great creature feeding on the roots of the yellow lilies, though others have seen that sight.

It is a little difficult to remember the past when on water, for water holds no trace of it. I have always known that the lumber rafts once came down the lake to the two sawmills, one here, and one at the Mills; but in our time the logs are towed a few at a time by a puffing old motor-boat or come in trucks lurching along the road. Once we met in the late fall a big yoke of oxen bringing logs; but that was nothing to the forty or fifty yoke Postmaster Sherman remembers seeing from the window of his house, coming single file over the ice. The lake is not used much in winter nowadays: a little ice is cut in square green blocks, a few cars take short cuts to their friends on the opposite shore, five winters ago a team was lost in a fault near Pint Pot Island just off our own shore. They had been working on this side of the lake, I forget now at what, and were going home to their farm across from us. In the middle of the pond between the two islands something went wrong. The ice buckled and broke under the heavy horses, and the man sprang back only just in time.

But it was not until Mrs. Hill came to help us last fall while Grace was home with a wrenched knee that I talked with someone who had known the lake intimately in its working days. Both her father and her husband had been lumber dealers over between Hamilton and Liberty Hill. She is quite an elderly woman, and she remembers how, when spring came on, her mother always made sure that she had some good strong new sheets. Then some morning long before dawn the rafts would put out, all along the shore, one or two from a farm. The logs were fastened to-gether in a great oblong—not pointed into a prow—and two or three of the sheets were fastened, each between two poles ("No, they didn't tear," Mrs. Hill assured me), for impromptu sails. Each raft had at least two men with poles and a long steering sweep, and she and her mother would stand on the shore watching the moving lanterns and listening to the shouting of the men from raft to raft.

"Mother always packed up a big pail of food for each one of the rafts," Mrs. Hill told me. "She was a fine cook, and they used to send good hearty food with the men in those days. There'd be a cold roast of beef or pork, and a loaf or two of bread and a crock of butter and maybe a pound of cheese and pies baked the day before, and a cake or two. The men would get to the Mills sometime during the afternoon, and all drive back together. But the early start gave them good appetites, and my mother never stinted them."

Chapter 23

LAST WEEK the annual auction and fair was held on the lawns of the County Home for Old People above the river. The first thing put up for sale was the plaster-of-Paris head of a young girl, smiling, with her face tilted towards an upraised shoulder. It went for sixty cents, but although I had no impulse to bid on it I was reminded of a queer little romance a friend once told me about. I heard the story here in Maine although the scene took place in another state; and as its touching quality is universal I venture to repeat it.

As a child and a young girl my friend always had a great many charming necklaces, given to her by her grandfather who lived alone in a big house with his servants, his wife having died, and his children having married and moved away. The old man's favorite possession was the bust of a laughing girl which stood in his study. Like the one sold the other day, it was a little less than life size.

This bust always interested his granddaughter because it wore a necklace looped up at the back, as the marble girl's neck was smaller than a living girl's would have been. Sometimes the necklace was of beads, or it might be of ivory painted to imitate roses, or of links of tortoise shell. Whatever the old gentleman found most feminine and fashionable, he bought for his statue; and the discarded

necklace was given to his granddaughter. I do not know
how many years this romance continued, but I hope that
it lasted the old man for his time. Life is illusion, the phi-
losophers say, and a memory, a dream, or perhaps a marble
bust in a study will do very well to keep an aging heart
sweet and sound.

Chapter 24

W<small>E LOOKED</small> carefully at the stoves, got into our warm coats, hats, and mittens, and went out. Our snowshoes stood patiently on their tails in the snowbank by the door and with them strapped to our feet, the banked hill slope was easily descended. The lake looked like a marble eye, white and expressionless. We crunched across it, the rackets of our snowshoes leaving two pretty, precise patterns of tracks in the snow behind us. They were like leaves criss-crossed in Jacobean embroidery, growing on an invisible vine, except when I blurred the pattern by stopping to tighten a strap.

It was a March day, but the thaw had not come yet. I think it must have been early March. There were no white lids of snow on the dark pine trees, no tracks on the level snow of the lake. From where we walked we could see or be seen by no house. We seemed to be in a clearing of the forest, entirely alone, with no other sound than the squeak of leather and the crunching of the snow.

At the opposite bank we climbed steeply to the rail-road track and negotiated with care a barbed-wire fence. We were now in the Bremens' pasture with its huge soli-tary oaks. Climbing still, we came to the hayfields, and so to the house and its two large barns. I don't remember where we met Lambert. Probably Laddie, the collie, barked, and Lambert came out of the big yellow cow barn. I know that he took us in there, and that the cows looked sleek and lazy in the tie-up, and that then he led us down a wide ramp to the cellar under the barn. It was lined with stone, had narrow windows under the ceiling and was filled with crowding sheep. Laddie went among them barking, and they moved about, keeping their staring eyes turned towards him. From the flock there arose the bleating of newborn lambs. Two or three had already been dropped—weak small things uttering weak small cries and covered with skins infinitely large and wrinkled. They were not pretty, they were not gay; but they touched me more than any skipping lamb I have ever seen in a green field. They were the first younglings of spring, born here under the ground, while the snow lay deep above them. At the moment they seemed like the epitome of all the roots and bulbs which strove in the darkness for the sun: they were hope in the womb of earth.

Lambert took us to the house later to see his mother, who gave us hot gingerbread and glasses of milk, and we talked for a little; but the early dusk was already beginning, and we soon made our excuses and started for home by the way we had come. When we reached the lake, where now the snow lay blue in the dimming light, we found that another pattern had been added to the double vine left by our snowshoes. Now the pad tracks of an animal went along close beside them. Beginning at our bank of the lake some large four-footed creature had followed our trail all the way across. So must the track of a scouting wolf have looked. Of course there are no wolves; but we had never seen a dog on the lake, nor could we imagine what dog this one might be, so large and so persistent in its interest in us.

This small puzzle was one never to be answered. The woods are mysterious. They enfold the Maine farms, and all sorts of things come out of them: innocent things like the young porcupine which has recently been eating high-top apples every afternoon while we have tea at the table below; pretty things like the deer which came with a herd of cows into the barn of a farmer near Hamilton, and which stayed with them winter and summer for nearly three years. And then there are other things neither innocent nor pretty. The summer before we went over to see the lambs, we had heard the Bremen sheep bleating steadily from their pasture. Our telephone was working then, and we rang up Lambert to ask him if anything were wrong, for we knew that the wind would carry the sound our way and not his.

"I'll go right down and see," he said.

A few days later we heard the story. He found the flock huddled in a wall corner, and one sheep dead. It had been recently killed. He did not examine it closely, but drove the flock up to the field near his house where he could keep an eye on them, and it was not until the next day that he had time to return to the carcass. In the meantime the killer had been back. The sheep had been eaten, bones and all. Only the skull and skin were left.

"No dog could have cracked big bones like that," Lambert said thoughtfully. "Nothing I know of could, unless it was a bear, or a Canada lynx."

Again came that thoughtful pause.

"Aren't any of those around here either," he admitted. "But in September they travel sometimes. You can't tell what may come out of the woods."

"Is it likely to come back for more sheep?" we asked.

"Well, it might, unless it's going some place," Lambert said.

But the killer was never heard of again in our parts. It had struck once, and then vanished. No one ever knew what it was.

Chapter 25

W E WERE DRIVING along the highway with our thoughts preceding us to the pleasant house in the next village where we were going for dinner, and to the people we should see there. We were in festive mood. The brightness had gone out of the sky: that sense of coolness, of evening, of lights and laughter to come was upon us. At first we scarcely noticed the cars parked in the long grass by the side of the road, but then we saw men with shotguns over their arms climbing the fence and starting off cautiously into the pine woods beyond. It looked as though they might be deer-hunting; but the season was not yet on, nor had we ever seen deer-hunting gone at in so concerted a manner. The woods we knew well—a very beautiful stand of pine with little underbrush, bounded on three sides by the river and on the fourth by the highway. The highway side was well guarded: by the hunters, by watching small boys, by people in parked cars, and now by the stocky form of a state policeman swinging off his motorcycle to join the crowd. As for the other three sides of the woods, the river was swift, wide, and deep.

A sort of chill came over us. When you see the hunters you think of the hunted. Almost hesitantly we asked someone what they were after.

"Man got out of jail this morning. He had a duplicate

key to a warden's car; but the warden had noticed something phony, and had his lock changed just yesterday. They think maybe he had clothes hidden somewhere and has been hitch-hiking towards Boston. A man in a Massachusetts car saw someone go into these woods, and they think they have him covered."

Oh, that man in a Massachusetts car! Where in Maine doesn't he turn up, driving too fast, crowding people half off the road, returning from our woods with dead deer slung head-downwards on his mudgards?

"A man with a Massachusetts license" did this or did that, said this or said that, reported one thing or another!

We drove on, our holiday mood blighted. Not that we don't believe in prisons; but there is something so primitive and fierce in a man hunt that even the glimpse of one is enough to take the lightness out of lighter affairs. However, we had a pleasant evening and some hours later retraced our road.

The man from Massachusetts was, as often, wrong. No one had entered the wood, or at least no one had hidden there. The hunters had tramped through every thicket and looked behind every boulder. There was no cover there for any quarry, and the amateur man hunters had gone home to their dinners. The convict had not, however, been forgotten. The road, opening out before our headlights, took us over several bridges, some long and some short. At every one of them a police car lurked, drawn back from the highway, its lights out, a watchful man tense at the wheel, studying each car that passed. We would see the gleam of starlight on a gray car bonnet, the faint shine of glass and metal, and the dark hulk of a figure inside. All night long, as patient as a wildcat on a branch, the hunters waited by the trail; but in the morning we learned that the watch had been in vain.

The convict for whom they were looking had not gone more than a hundred yards from the familiar walls of the jail. When hunger, thirst, and weariness had subdued him, he gave himself up.

Chapter 26

O NE OF THE strangest and most interesting visitors we ever had at the farm was a sewing woman, who for some summers toured the New England coast in a little car, stopping at each village for a week or two to make curtains and slip covers for people who found such work hard to get done. We have no sewing machine at the farm, so she did not stay with us as I wish she might have done; we only saw her as she knelt by the old red plush chair taking measurements, or stood by the white iron bedsteads snipping out patterns in newspaper for the slip covers which were to hide the iron and transform it. She talked well and with charm, a charm which was part of her face and her carriage and the big floppy hat she wore and the loose gloves she pulled off as she entered the door. She was elderly; it was hard to say just how old, for every motion she made was light and swift, and she had that assurance which makes me think of the old French duchess who said, when asked her formula for youth, "Oh, I have always been loved, and eaten fresh vegetables."

That charm, that seasoned gayety, that knowledge that one is respected and safe from slights and indifference— those are somehow rare things in America among the old. But she had them. She seemed to be without bitterness or fear, and her stories were delightful.

She showed us on the second visit (the visit with pins and fittings-on, that was) a photograph of herself in a habit and derby, riding side-saddle on a good horse. She was still very fond of riding, she said; and that led us to talk of horses and of the old days. When she was a child, her father had been the Wells Fargo agent in New York. She was an only daughter, and he made a great pet of her.

"Fanny," he said one morning, "come down to the office around eleven. Sitting Bull will be there."

In those days the railroads once a year gave free tickets to New York to the chiefs through whose lands the tracks passed, so that they might do their tribal shopping in blankets, beads, red flannel, and kettles. Her father took charge of them while they were in New York. Little Fanny was not unaccustomed to seeing feathered headbands in his office nor to hearing the soft slip of moccasins on his floors, but when she came in that morning dressed in her little bonnet and pelisse she met a glance of a dignity she had never met with before. Sitting Bull, with several lesser chiefs, was waiting for her father to be free to go with them to the shops which catered to the Indian trade. The old chief took her up on his buckskinned knee and talked to her. He gave the child some keepsake (I do not remember what now—perhaps a beaded bag), and later she stood on tiptoe at the office window watching her father walking down the street beside Sitting Bull, hearing the heavy wheels of the drays, and the stir of the coals in the stove behind her.

When she was sixteen her father took the family for a summer in Colorado. Fanny bought a horse for very little, because its tail was quite bare of any hairs and most buyers would not look twice at such a scarecrow. But it was a wonderful horse, fast, sure-footed, and easy-gaited. It had been a squaw's horse and was trained to kneel when it was to be mounted. Besides that, it would allow no man near it. Neither her father nor her brother could ride it, but it was perfectly gentle with her.

All summer she rubbed its tail with ointments; and by fall the hairs were grown in again, and there was no difficulty in selling her wonderful horse for twice what she had paid for it.

If she told us more, I don't remember it. Sitting Bull stalking down old Canal Street, the squaw horse kneeling to be mounted, remain in my mind with the exotic charm of the black-eyed Susans which grow wild now in our fields, but which Henry tells me are really prairie flowers which have worked their way eastward against the tide of immigration as the land has been cleared of forest between them and the sea. I never look at them without a faint sense of the buffalo herds, and of Indian tepees by a brown river; and so, when I think of the itinerant sewing woman, I see a shadow behind her of the West before it was quite tamed. But she herself chugged up our lane a third time quite casually, put on the slip covers she had made for beds and chairs, and, tilting her great hat and drawing on her driving gloves, drove away to return no more—neither to our farm nor to any of the villages which she had once visited like a migrating and solitary bird.

Chapter 27

"I KNEW him myself," the young soldier on the train told Henry. "It seemed funny to us kids. He was just like the rest of us most of the time, but in a heavy rain he'd kind of go loony. He'd jump up and down and wave his arms and make queer noises. Yes, you could say like barking, like the barking of a seal. He wouldn't come in while the rain lasted unless someone went out and pulled him in."

Henry of course likes folk stories as much as I do, and this was all from a neighboring town.

"Like a seal?" he asked.

The young man looked at Henry, wondering whether he would be believed if he went on. Then he said:

"His mother, you see, was the wife of a keeper at a lighthouse on one of the islands. She was on the water one day coming from the Main when a big seal suddenly poked his head up out of a wave near her and barked. She was going to have a baby, and she'd never cared for seals. She was startled, and the baby was kind of marked by the seal, as they call it."

Henry nodded with full understanding. He believes in a world where lots of things can't be explained, where one lives side by side with the unknown. Perhaps that is one reason why he likes the country. The past is much more living to people's minds on the farms: they go by the signs of the weather, and remember what their grandfathers and grandmothers used to think. Everything is not explained for them in the latest scientific jargon, so incisive and assured, though next week the whole theory may be junked for one quite opposite. No, in the country, people watch the sun and the moon and study the wind as they did ten thousand years ago. And the men judge the coming winter by the depth to which the angleworms have dug, and the whiteness of the chickens' breastbones; and the women say that the cake fell because they were worried about something and only a light heart can bake a light cake, or that the hyacinth didn't bloom because they'd used a new pot, and should have remembered that no hyacinth can thrive in any but an old one.

And they watch how the cats and the cattle act, or the swallows, to foretell a storm, and see on which side of the islands the slick water stretches to judge the direction of the wind; and they listen to what kind of song the robin is singing, for if it is saying "Scour your skillets, scour your skillets, scour your skillets," there'll be no haying the next day.

Living very close to nature, the farms live very close to wonder. There are many things they can't explain, but for them a child is "marked" for some reason and not by accident.

Grace's niece, for instance, when carrying a baby, went to a cupboard; and when she opened it, there sat a little brown-gray mouse with its tail hanging down over the shelf. She put her hand to her throat in the gesture common to most women when startled, and after the mouse scurried away thought nothing more about it. But some force had been set to work, and when her little son was born he had the picture of a mouse on his throat, gray-brown, with the little tail hanging down just as his mother had seen it in her cupboard.

I have never read Holmes's *Elsie Venner*, but I know it is the story of a girl who had been marked by a snake. And I remember the tale of a friend of mine who went to a back-country hamlet to teach soon after she had graduated from normal school. Her winter was eerie, to say the least. She boarded with a pleasant middle-aged couple and their very commonplace son. But there was another son living in town who was by no means commonplace. I'll take him up later. Her room was on the ground floor opposite the shack of an old crazy man who always went about everywhere with a little yellow dog on a string. The old man took a great fancy to the new teacher; he was also devoted to his dog. Somehow he got the idea that there was enmity between the two, and it was only by good luck that it was the little dog he strangled and not the girl.

After that she was afraid to stay alone in the house when the family went visiting. Whatever the hour at which they might return home, and however dull the visit might appear, she always accepted their invitation to go along. But the family itself had its peculiarities. The mother explained. As a young married woman, she had been going out into the woodshed when a big snake slithered across the floor ahead of her. When her first son was born it was clear he had been marked. He was as much like a snake as a man, the mother said, speaking with a mixture of loathing and fascination.

After that my friend used to watch the young man when he came to the house for Sunday dinner, and she could certainly see what his mother meant. Where the rest of the family were stocky and heavy-boned, he was thin, supple and appeared to be almost without joints. His black hair was combed sleekly down on a rather queerly shaped head, and she never saw his eyelids close over his unwinking gaze. She thought that he was rather proud of his distinction and played up to it, and that certain snakelike motions of his head were perhaps conscious; but the effect was distinctly unpleasant. Altogether she was not sorry when her first year of teaching was over and she was moved to another school and a less charged neighborhood.

Well, I don't know, myself. Why does the simpleminded man of our village sit on the curb with the tears running down his face when the moon is full? Why do people die along the coast when the tide turns to the ebb? Do plants thrive better for someone who loves them? I don't know the answers, but our neighbors do not question such obvious facts as these.

Chapter 28

Ellen is one of the best story-tellers I have ever known, racy, humorous, tolerant, and pitying. She lives in a near-by town which for me flashes with light from a thousand strange facets:

"I first saw her one day on the train. I couldn't help noticing that she was reading a French book and was middle-aged and very well dressed. We got into talk, and she told me that she lived all by herself in a house in the woods: it was only later I heard that years ago she'd been run out of town . . .

" 'Yes,' my tenant remarked, 'that man walks too straight to be honest.' And at that time he was greatly respected by everyone. It was only much later that it came out . . .

"They hadn't spoken for years but that night the neighbors heard scream after scream from his room . . .

"And she insisted on going to the church in a taxi. Though the church was only a block from the house. It wouldn't do to have the groom call for her in his car, either. He mustn't see the bride on their wedding day, you know—even if they *had* been already living together all winter . . .

"And she called out: 'Damn you! Come in.' And when

she saw it was a neighbor she said: 'Oh, excuse me! I thought it was Mother.'

"So at last the professor put his head out of the window and yelled, 'My God, madam, can't you remember that you're a widow?' "

I remember the stories, or sometimes only snatches of them, each a New England novel compressed into five minutes of talk over a teacup. But most of these stories are a little too urban and recent for my use. I like the tale which has been stored like an apple in the attic, and has felt the cold of winter crackling the shingles overhead and heard the big stupid black flies of spring bumbling and bungling at the dusty windows. Perhaps I like fields in the picture—the houses in a town, even a little town, come too close: the lines warp one another into bitter shapes. These thwarted, desperate, funny stories have not the quiet comedy and tragedy in them that our true farm stories keep. Here we are nearer the other world of wonder, the cows low for milking, the fox barks from the autumn woods, there is a ring around the moon.

But this friend knows country stories, too. She took us one day for a picnic on a road which was barely passable. It was hard to believe that this lane dipping down to streams in the wood, veering over rocky ledges, had once been the stage coach road; and it was not easy to think that the little deserted red-brick building opposite the graveyard at a forgotten crossing had ever been a tavern.

But she assured us that it had. We took out our rugs and picnic things and spread them in the sun. There were apples very bright in the old trees, and the biggest and most perfect spiderwebs I have ever seen were spread across the open doorways of the gray sheds. The inevitable chipmunk came chittering and scolding along a stone wall, and the crickets were making their usual scarcely heard chorus.

We walked about the little building, past the clumps of lilacs, and climbed on a cellar bulkhead, trying to peer through a shutter into the dark interior.

The bulkhead reminded Ellen of something.

"It was down here," she remarked casually, "that they kept the Eskimos that winter."

It was as though she had said, "In this room they boarded the tiger." Not of course that Eskimos are dangerous; but here in these deserted fields they seemed as exotic as anything from the jungle. I looked at the little tavern with a new excitement. Only two or three narrow peeps of glass lighted whatever cellar there was under the house; but Ellen said that the Eskimos preferred it to a room. It must have been more like an igloo.

I have read the story since with names and dates and later happenings, but I prefer to remember it as Ellen told it while we unpacked the picnic basket in the late September sunshine. It took place in that wonderful time "when the old people I first knew here were children." Some vessel—was it a sealer?—had found a group of Eskimos on an ice floe, drifting south; I rather think there was a white man with them, an English explorer. Anyway, there were several Eskimo men with their women, and two or three children as well. They were taken aboard, and then the question arose as to what to do with them, as it was too late in the season to go north again to any land they knew. A local skipper agreed to take them with him in the spring when he went. Meanwhile he suggested this old tavern, where he could make arrangements, and the winter was likely to be cold enough to keep the Arctic visitors comfortable. And so it turned out. They lived for months in this dark hole about which we prowled. I wonder if they built an entrance to it of packed snow, and whether they were given whale oil to burn in its cold depths? At least none of them died. And the old people of the town, who then were children, remember them walking occasionally into the village to make a few simple purchases, wearing their fur-trimmed parkas and sealskin boots, and still tell how round-faced and bright-eyed the Eskimo children were.

And then in the spring they sailed away, and the memory of them became a legend and things were dated for a while from "the winter the Eskimos were here," and gradually they were forgotten as a visit of Arctic owls would be forgotten; but Ellen had heard the story from people who had seen them, and she told it to me just as I am telling you.

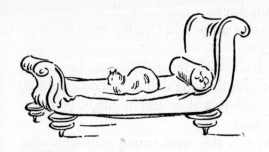

Chapter 29

Mrs. Hardy's grandfather as a young man lived on the neighboring neck, and his sweetheart lived on Snackety at the end of the pond where there are only cellar holes now, and old apple trees in overgrown fields where the deer bed in the uncut grass after they have eaten their fill of old-fashioned apples, whose very names have probably been forgotten. The road a few years ago was still passable to a bold driver. There was one truck which used that haunted short cut, but I doubt if anyone could get through now. I have seen a fox in a field there which is still cut, and an eagle soar up with white head and tail spread like a shining fan. But except for the animals, a few hunters, and the haymakers in July, no one comes to Snackety any more, and the graves, grown over with pines, are unvisited.

But when Mrs. Hardy's grandfather was a boy Snackety was a thriving mile of road with farms all along it, and there his sweetheart lived.

He started off to call on her one Sunday afternoon; but his luck was out, and he met with the tithingman.

"Where are you going?" asked the tithingman.

"Mr. Hussey's," says the young man.

"And what may your business at Mr. Hussey's be?" asked the tithingman.

Perhaps he already knew.

At any rate the young suitor told him the truth.

"To see his daughter."

That settled it. Back with the tithingman he had to go, and kick his heels for the long dull afternoon until sunset brought the Sabbath to a close and he might go courting as much as he liked.

I am sorry to add that this same young man who went courting on the Sabbath became in his turn conventional, and whipped his son for fishing on Sunday. What the boy never forgot or forgave, however, was that his father took the fine string of lake trout he'd brought up from the pond —our lake had trout in those days—and gave it to his married sister who had driven over from town to visit for the day. If the fish had been thrown on the dung heap, the matter would have ended there; but the memory of the thrashing coupled with the thrifty saving of the fish rankled in that boy's mind all his life. So when he grew up he did not in his turn become conventional. It was he who twitted the minister, hunted foxes, and worked on whatever day of the week he saw fit.

"Many a load of hay has been brought into this barn on a Sunday," says old Mrs. Hardy, nodding and smiling. "In my father's time, and in Walter's too. We're not superstitious."

Well, the tradition against farm work on Sunday is certainly more than superstition; but whatever it is it has had to give way to circumstance in these days when so many of the farmers are working at the shipyards, and must get the hay in on Sundays or never. The feeling about Friday, however, could be classed with superstition purely, and the "farmers on the other side of the pond" shared it with all sailors. They didn't like to begin any project on a Friday. Mrs. Hardy told us one evening of a farmer "over there" who had a fine bull calf he wanted to use as a steer. The man who owned the sawmill at that time happened to have another one, that would make a justabout perfect match for it in size, color, and general shape.

The farmer spent some weeks in dropping in to see the sawmill calf, bargaining for it, and at last the two men reached an agreement.

The farmer was delighted, "Let's see," he said, "how old did you say he was?"

"He'll be nine weeks this Friday," replied the sawmill owner.

A change came over the purchaser's face.

"Here, give me that money back," he cried, "I haven't a lick of use for a steer as was born Friday."

Chapter 30

Iᴛ ᴡᴀꜱ ᴏɴᴇ of those nights when you know things are
wrong," Mary Hutton said. "The wind began blowing ter-
ribly from the southeast, and one of the maids and I got
up and went about, closing and latching the windows to
keep them from banging. You could feel the house shake,
and it went on and on.

"In the morning I had the horses harnessed and drove
over to Pocassett Point. I knew there'd have been trouble
there. And I was right. Two fishing boats had been lost
one after another off the lighthouse. You know how the
point runs out there, all rock and rockweed. Fifteen men
had been drowned, and they had a row of bodies down in
the boathouse, and my nephew went in to see them; but I
didn't feel like it. There had been three men saved, who'd
got up above the waves on the rock—an awful thing to
have to do in the night with the breakers pounding on
stone. I talked with one of the survivors. He was sunk. I
don't think I ever saw a man more upset than he was. It
seems that, as he was just getting his hands on some rockweed to try to make his landing on the next wave, he felt
something come up near him, and a hand gripped his
shoulder. He didn't know who it was. But the weight began tearing him loose from his hold on the weeds. He

knew he didn't have any chance of getting out with the weight of two men, so he reached out and tore the hand off his shoulder. With the next wave he managed to get ashore, he didn't know how. But I tell you he was sunk, thinking about that hand and wondering which man it had belonged to. Of course anyone could understand how he felt. Listening to him, I felt badly myself. And next winter I happened to read that those three men had all been frozen to death in a gale off Cape Cod."

Chapter 31

THE HOUSE next door to us, the last house on the lane, is a fine, rather stark late eighteenth century farm with a big locust tree in front of it. The barn is across the lane, and has the same fine stern lines. Seen from any direction, but especially from the pond below, they make a noble brace of buildings. When we first came here the place had a deserted air; the clapboards were gray and slipping from place, and perhaps one or two of the windows were broken. But we were told that the last member of the family still came back to it occasionally, and that there was a fine upstairs chamber fully furnished, with an open fireplace and a carved cupboard in the corner.

I laugh when I think how these facts stirred my imagination, how desolate I pictured the rest of the great house, how exquisite that one southwest chamber. I imagined the owner returning by night—as in fact he usually did after a day of business in Boston. I saw him seated abstractedly before a fire in a room of almost sybaritic beauty, a pipe in his mouth, his eyes on the flames which rose on the hearth at his feet. I was sure that he wore a brocaded dressing gown, and that a fine leather-bound book rested on his knee as he mused. The first evening I saw those windows actually shining across the darkness of the fields, I felt as though we were very near to the stuff of which British novels were once made.

However, the truth was much simpler and more matter-of-fact. Soon the young man brought his bride to the old farm, and we saw the whole house, far less bare than I had supposed in the downstairs rooms grouped about the great central fireplace, and far less elaborate in that one chamber, which at that time was the only finished room upstairs, the rest being one great unfinished attic in which children, apples, trunks, and hired help might be stored indefinitely. Our own house used to have the same arrangement but had been changed before we saw it, as the big house itself has more recently been. The moth-gray clapboards have been repaired and painted white. There are window boxes at the windows, and smoke rises from the great pink-red chimney until late into the fall. But still there are two or three details which set this Hill farm apart. For instance, in 1791 it was moved across the pond. I don't know how anyone had the courage to build such a large civilized house in the wilderness in 1791, in a clearing surrounded by forest, bears, and Indians; but once it was built I can't imagine how they had the courage to move it.

Then on a beam in the barn there is carved a sailboat. I like that. It must have been done long ago by some boy dreaming of the sea from which the sea gulls and fogs come drifting in. And, thirdly, on the attic stairs there is a repeated scorched mark as though a very hot poker had been dragged down their length. That scar was left by a lightning stone which rolled down the back stairs when the house was empty during a bad storm thirteen years ago. For I wonder it did no further harm. And, last of all, one summer the mistress of the house used occasionally to meet a four-foot-long milk snake in the attic, where it had gone apparently ratting. A great snake is mysterious and rather terrifying. She was glad when this one returned to more normal caves and passages in the earth, and no longer slid up between their walls and slithered across the floor above their sleeping heads. But its presence is one more item to set the farm a little apart.

I suppose the thing about the Hill farm which makes it really important to us is that it is the last house on the road. It backs against the wilderness, the lake, the wooded hills beyond. Even when empty it stands between us and the full sweep and force of the north, of the Arctic. It is an outpost, a thing made by man, set about by apple trees and walls, where generations have lived.

And then it is the parent farmhouse, from which ours is derived, when the inheritance was divided and the land shared between two sons. Our graveyard under the two maples at the top of the hayfields holds the dead of both farms, and there have never been walls dividing the pasture and woodlands from each other. The pastures are returning to pine, and this year none of the three Hill's Neck farms has succeeded in finding men to cut the hay. As Mrs. Hardy said last week, voicing that fear which is in every farmer's heart in these farms at the edge of the woods, "I guess the Neck is going back to the wilderness."

When the man power of a farm fails with sickness or age or death or absence, the women watch the farm sink away as water sinks away into sand. I shall never forget a call we once made on an old woman living by herself in a little house farther down the lake. She was so crippled by rheumatism that she walked doubled over. It was not until she sat slowly and painfully down, that one saw how handsome and vital her face was. Her house was spotless. Every chair had a starched doily on the seat and another across the back which must be washed and starched again after each visitor. Somehow Miss Annie Wise swept even her cobwebs away from the corners of the ceilings. Crippled though she was, her will was indomitable. The house had not changed within from the standards she had known in her girlhood. But beyond the door she was powerless. I can remember how she crept over beside us as we stood looking out of a window across the fields to the lake. I remember her deep, violent, and musical voice crying out from a mouth held scarcely above the window sill:

"I'm glad my father ain't alive to see them young pines growing in his fields!"

Since the Civil War killed so many of the young men and the West drew away so many more to the rich prairie earth, that has been the cry deep in the heart of the people who are left, trying to hold the farms to their duty, to compel the fields to yield their service:

"We're glad our fathers can't see the young pines growing in their fields!"

Chapter 32

Aﬀter many years of life I still feel a stranger to this universe, constantly surprised, often enchanted by unexpected small facts and sights, and frequently saddened by the course of its affairs and unable to accept tranquilly the cruelties of existence. But sometimes they come, so softened and shadowed by time, that even tragedy takes on a certain charm. I feel that charm when Maud talks about her great-great-uncle, the hunchback.

Maud lives in a big white house with wide verandas spilling over with wicker chairs, children, and dogs. There are lawns going down to the river and three Indians lie buried on the knoll across from the flower garden. In the cellar of the house one great stone is always kept whitewashed. The tradition is that it revolves and opens onto a passage leading down to the river, where in truth there is another flat stone with a staple in it set against the face of the bank. The whitewash is still freshly applied to the stone from year to year, but no one, even among Maud's eight boys and girls, has ever succeeded in turning the white stone and disclosing the passage. The secret, if there is a secret, has been lost.

Before the house became the charming place of open fires and fine casual furniture that it is today, it was Maud's grandmother's farm.

"I've often heard the family tell of my great-great-uncle," she says. "He was a hunchback, and the girl he loved when he was young would not marry him. He had a negro slave whom he bought off one of the ships which came here in those days. My grandmother remembered this slave as a very old black man. As this great-great-uncle grew older he grew more and more irritable and difficult, a crabbed, miserable old man. He had a great horror that someone would dig him up when he was dead, to study his body for its deformity, and in his will he left a provision that there should be no headstone on his grave but only an unmarked millstone laid flat across it, and that two men should guard it day and night."

In due time the hunchback died and was buried and the millstone was laid across his grave. For two and a half years —so long as his money lasted—two men guarded his grave, in rain and sunshine, in snow and hail. All night, in all kinds of weather, a lantern shone there, back of the house in the small family cemetery plot. One wonders what the men talked about, what jokes they made to while away the time, what bits of village gossip were exchanged across that millstone. There must have been minor epics of endurance lived through when the temperature was cracking the trees at twenty-five below zero. I suppose they built fires or passed in and out frequently to the kitchen for a thawing-out and a hot drink of something, probably rum and water.

At the end of two and a half years the hunchback's money was gone, and the men could return to their haying and woodcutting without the curious intervals in the quiet graveyard.

"But I remember," said Maud, "that we children always

thought it was funny that out of the hole in the middle of the millstone a thorn tree grew."

And when she took us to see the grave, there the thorn tree still was, its trunk filling the hole, its thorny branches spreading over the great round of the stone, and its roots growing, as in the old ballads, from the dust which had been the sad sour heart of the hunchback.

Pocassett Harbor was the scene of much fighting during the French and Indian wars, and the fort changed hands several times. A pirate named Bull once sailed up the river and attacked the town. Now it is a quiet place, with the rebuilt fort, an old garrison house, and an older graveyard to mark its past, and a few modern houses and a couple of piers where one may order boiled lobsters and eat them at long tables with the sandwiches and coffee which the wise bring for themselves.

It is less than an hour's drive from the farm, and we go there several times a summer, enjoying the different mood of the coast. The sea water sparkles and shines, like a thousand thousand minnows showing their silver sides to the sun. The islands look artificial on their platforms of rock, with their spruce woods clipped neatly by the wind. A lighthouse has the air of a freshly painted toy, and one can hear the mournful tolling of a bell buoy on a reef rocked by the swells. The gulls are an endless study in beauty and greed. They soar down from the sky or sit like ducks on the water about the piers waiting for the lobster shells to be thrown into the sea. Hoarse complaints, wild squabbles ensue; often enough a gull swims off, well weighted down at the bow with its share, its sharp neat stern pointing upwards. Or the gulls wade along the rocks collecting starfish. Suddenly a strong white head and Roman beak disappear under water, there is a sharp tug, and up comes the head again with a star at its tip, which is eaten with frequent immersions to help wash it down.

The sea air has on sunny days a gayety about it, a wild invigoration commanding one to do something, to go somewhere, to seek the adventure just around the corner. No wonder so many men along the coast took to deep-sea voyages, and came to know all the great harbors of the world. In the little shops of Maine we have bought old trinkets from China, India, and Africa brought home by the local men. A man once told me that when he was a boy the little town he grew up in on the opposite side of Pocassett Point was filled with monkeys and parrots from the Gold Coast. I myself have seen rings and ivory tusks and carved wooden combs brought back in that trade; we know that one bold skipper hoped to bring Marie Antoinette, the Queen of France, back to Wiscasset. There was no end to the importations!

Opposite the town of Pocassett Harbor, on a slope of land looking straight down the river to the islands and the sea, there stands a large square house, well back from the road, behind an ornamental fence. There is a summer house to one side in a thicket of flowering bushes; a golden centaur weathervane tops it, his arrow pointing towards the sky. The big house is empty now. Its lawns are uncut, its garden forgotten; but even today it is the very epitome of a Maine sea captain's house.

Andy Taggett told us its story. The captain was a relative of his—I should only be guessing if I put a name to that cousinship or great-unclehood, but he was "in the family." Like so many of the men who went to sea as boys, he was a captain in his twenties, and by forty was prepared to marry and settle down to a life ashore. His young wife had a terror of the sea, and the captain gave her a solemn promise that he would make no more voyages after they were married.

So the wedding took place and the bride came to live in the big square house over Pocassett Harbor, and a baby was either born or was to come. And then, like a voice from the sea, came a letter from the owners in New York. For some reason one of their vessels was without a captain. They understood that the man to whom they were writing had retired—but would he not make just one more trip for them? It was a summer voyage, a mere nothing, but it would be a great favor to them until they could make other arrangements, etc., etc.

Was the captain yearning for the sea after a year ashore? Would a vessel and sailors and the sound of wind in the rigging be welcome after months of his wife's talk and the tinkle of her piano, and visits among the neighbors, or sober work in the garden? Or, loath to go, did he feel the call of duty to his former employers?

We only know that he went to his wife and got from her permission to retract his promise for this one voyage. Was it given unwillingly, I wonder, or was she reassured by the fact that this was to be a summer venture? At all events, she allowed her husband to go. The promise was to be in abeyance.

It is hardly necessary to end the story. If we were ancient Greeks we should say that Nemesis cared nothing for patchwork amendments. The oath had been given and broken. Summer voyage or not, the captain never returned from it, and all the bride's forebodings came true. Never again did the big square house hear its master's footsteps at the door; never again did he stride down the gravel walk to the summerhouse overlooking the harbor and the sea; he was not there to watch his son grow into manhood.

Chapter *Chapter* 34

I<small>T</small> w<small>AS</small> a summer Sunday morning, and we were driving
up the river from the bridge, past the great square-pillared
mansion that looks down the green tide rip of the river to
the twin towns at the head of navigation. It is a wonderful
example of the Greek revival house of the 1840's, with a
very beautiful fence. We knew it was empty and had been
for some time. It was undoubtedly at my suggestion that
Henry stopped the car and we walked up the weed-grown
path, and stood under the square pillars looking down the
river. After exclaiming over the beauty of the scene, which
though part of the villages is also part of the great natural
sweep of the tides and the life of the river, we turned
humanly enough to look into the double parlors through
the long French windows beside us. But we saw more than
we had bargained on, for there looking out at us, as close
to the inside of the window as we were to the outside, was
the long distinguished face and the long lean body, dressed
in a white linen suit with a flower in the buttonhole, of the
owner of the place. He, too, had dropped in for a Sunday
visit, but with a good deal more right than we. However,
he flung open a door and invited us in. The parlors were
twin rooms, with marble fireplaces and Brussels carpets.
Curtainless and high-ceilinged, they were rather austere,

as the rooms in many Greek revival houses are. It was easy to read the tastes of many masters there. A stuffed bobcat and raccoon stood on the bookcases; a caribou head leaned wistful and curious from the wall above the piano, and a rack made from the horns of various types of deer and gazelles waited for coats and hats in the wide hallway. We had heard that the man who was showing us about could walk through any woods at night without sound and without hitting into the trunk of a tree or the branches of a bush, that he knew the ways of all the birds and creatures.

"We used to be allowed three deer, two caribou, and one moose by the old game laws," he told us. "But the caribou are all gone now, shot off. The last herd was driven over a cliff on Katahdin. A pity they don't restock it sometime."

I can't remember where the elephant's-leg footstool had come from, with the hay bursting from the seams.

But perhaps you have an idea of the rooms—old-fashioned, long unused, smelling of dampness, and clearly belonging to men who had loved horses and hunting. In the second parlor, however, one came up short, before something very different. Between the long windows was a high cabinet with glass doors, apparently French or Italian. Inside and out, it was of buhl, dark tortoise-shell inlaid with gold and silver. There were designs of eagles, crowns, seraphs' heads, and intertwined monograms.

"I don't know anything about it," said its owner. "Don't care for that kind of thing myself, you know. Wouldn't read a book if you paid me. Rather look at something real any day. But I do know that after the Siege of Paris one of my grandfather's captains brought this back. Been in a palace or museum or something. Can't remember who it was made for. Oh, wait a minute. It's written down some-where."

He fished behind a red-lacquer Chinese vase on one of the shelves, found nothing, felt behind its mate, drew out a paper.

"H'm! Just as I thought, one of those French kings. Here, you can see for yourself."

There it was, made by—an Italian name which I forget —"for Mme. de Montespan by order of Louis XIV."

So there it was. We traced the monograms in gold and silver under the crowns. But our host was not much inter-ested.

"Don't care for that sort of thing myself," he repeated. "However, I was good and mad one day when I came in and found it moved halfway across the room. Neighbors told me a truck with two or three men had driven by here one evening. Neighbors didn't think anything about it at the time, but the men in the truck must have been after the cabinet. I waited for them with a shotgun for two or three nights, but they didn't come back. I guess they found it heavy. Don't care for it, as I said, but don't like to have my things stolen, either."

The buhl cabinet was back in its place in an empty house, above a vesselless river. We sighed, as we went out again to the sunlight and the high-pillared veranda.

Chapter 35

IT HAPPENED to be in a town on the St. Lawrence that we had dinner with a great-granddaughter of the man who had built the Greek revival house which overlooks the headwaters of the Taniscot.

"He went to sea when he was ten, was a captain at twenty, and retired at forty with a fleet of packets of his own. My mother used to go there as a little girl to visit. Her grandfather was old and growing forgetful then. Steam had replaced sail, and his packets were only pictures on the walls, but he lived on in the big house and used to like to have his married children and their children with him for long visits.

"There was one day my mother always remembered though she was only a little girl at the time. She was awakened at dawn by loud raps on the door. It was her grandfather going from room to room calling: 'Get up! Get up! There's a vessel coming up the river! Put on your best clothes to meet her.'

"Everyone knew that no vessel of his would ever come up the river again; but the old man was still master in his own house, and no one dared to disobey him. The servants were roused. Whispering and a little frightened, the young daughters dressed their children and themselves in their prettiest clothes and hurried downstairs. The old captain was dressed in his best and waiting. His tall silk hat and silver-headed cane ready on the table in the hall.

" 'Hurry! Hurry!' he kept calling. 'We can't be late! Hurry up, there!'

"Everyone looked rather white in the dawn light. The servants waited on the table with awestruck faces. After breakfast the old man hurried to the high veranda. The sun was shining there by then, striking in gently from the eastern sky.

"The captain looked down the river.

" 'She'll be along soon,' " he said, and sat down to wait.

"The daughters and their children stood about in little clusters and knots, waiting, too, they did not know for what. Then one of them saw that the old man had fallen asleep in the sun, his silver-headed cane across his knees. Perhaps this was what they were waiting for. On tiptoe they crept into the house and up the stairs, to change their clothes again, to take up their ordinary morning, leaving the old man, still asleep, facing down the river. When he woke up, he too changed his clothes. No mention was ever made of that early morning vigil. That was the last time that the captain ever waited for any of his vessels, but somehow my mother never forgot it."

Chapter 36

Richmond is a little forgotten town on the Kennebec
with two streets of fine houses parallel to the river and a
long history of ship-building, ship-sailing, and of the ice
trade behind it, and apparently very little ahead. Across
from it in the river lies Swan Island with its woods and
farms where legend says lived the lady sachem Jacataqua
who followed Aaron Burr to the siege of Quebec under
the leadership of that other controversial figure, Benedict
Arnold. I have never looked up the subject enough to
know how much of the tale is legend, and how much
"little" history, as the French say. What lies behind the
account of the bear and her cubs killed by Burr and the
young Indian girl? of the feast later and the toasts drunk
there? of her journey through the wilderness mountains
with the expedition, as official hunter? or of Burr's friend-
ship with a British officer met with by chance at a spring
in the forest in whose charge he put his Indian mistress
until her baby should be born? I have no idea if the beloved Theodosia Burr, the idol of her father's heart, who

perished so mysteriously somewhere off the coast of the Carolinas, perhaps walking a pirate's plank—I have no idea if she really *had* a half-sister, with long black hair and bright black eyes, whose mother's people were settled on Swan Island.

The most interesting thing we noticed there was a very large wooden arrow fastened as a weathervane to the top of a pine tree growing tall and shaggy on the bank. The arrow of course marked the wind on the river—and sometimes bodies of water seem to have their own winds differing from the land winds beside them. The arrow was so large, so old, and so noticeable that we remembered it when we came to talk with an old man later at the grocery store.

He was a relic of one of the great Maine trades, a retired blacksmith who had followed the camp meetings in summer and the ice cutters in winter. He remembered when a thousand buggies used to drive to the camp-meeting oaks back of the Schusters' at our own Hillsboro, and he told us that the farmers left baskets of high-top apples by the side of the road, while the worldly swapped stories and horses, and the religious listened to the preachers on the outdoor platforms under the trees. His more important work was in shoeing the horses that hauled ice on the Kennebec. Two things have handicapped the Maine farmer, he said: the introduction of artificial ice, and the replacement of the horsecar by the trolley. Until then, a hard-working man could count on a thousand dollars a season for pressed hay—that's why our barns are so large. If he needed more money he cut some ice and shipped it somewhere in sawdust. This old man had lived in the era when the local farmer not only made his own living but handled money. After we had talked for a while, we asked him about the weathervane.

"Oh that!" he said. "That was put up by Jim Dekker. His father was a captain, drowned before Jim come along. From the time Jim was a little boy he wanted to be a captain too; but his mother wouldn't ever let him go to sea. He certainly loved boats and anything to do with water. He had two stores here when he died, and was pretty comfortably fixed. But that wasn't what he'd really have liked if he'd had his own way.

"Funny thing about his will. He had a nice power-boat when he died. He left it fixed so that his heirs could salvage the engine and any of the gear they wanted. He didn't care about that. But the boat itself they was to take out into the channel and saw right in two. Yes, it was all in his will; right in two pieces, he wanted her, and sunk. He didn't intend anyone else should ever use his boat. She was the nearest he ever come to having a vessel of his own."

Chapter 37

W<small>E HAD</small> our lunch on a point at Day's Landing on the Kennebec opposite Bath but higher up the river. Near us there was a monument to the last family carried away into captivity by the French and Indians. Above us on the bank was the garrison house held by the grandfather of the children carried away. He later spent much time and money trying to ransom them. The stone records his success—now a boy, now a girl brought back; but some disappeared. One was taken to France and lived and died there. One wonders whether in Paris or in some provincial town, whether with a great family or with some weaver or baker, lived this little child who had awakened to flames and screams and the smell of rancid bear's grease long ago above the Kennebec.

I considered the possibility of making a story of it, turning it and its wonderful contrasts about in my mind; but I had already written one story of the captivities, and as we drove on I let the subject fade out of my thoughts. We were going upriver, now with broad magnificent views, now through farms or along stretches of road too far back from the river to see anything. We passed a small Quakerish farmhouse in a clearing which we knew was one of the several farms of Tristram Coffin, then followed the road on and on across bridges, across high land and low until we came to Munich Courthouse.

"I don't know if he will be here," said Ellen. "Last time I saw him, a year or two ago, he was not well. And he's quite elderly."

The house was a great one, four stories high, built for a variety of purposes. On one floor, court had been held; on another, the soldiers had been quartered; on the third, the family lived; and the fourth held the velvet-brown attics where the two daughters of the house had been kept for a period of several weeks—or was it months?— during the occupancy of the British. Behind the house an old lawn stretched to a high arborvitae hedge so thick that one could not see the river just beyond it.

We tapped on the door of the kitchen ell, and the master himself opened the door and invited us in to where he had been sitting by the wide kitchen hearth. It was growing cold with autumn. We sat watching the flames while he entertained us courteously. He guessed that we would like to see the house where he camped among the ghosts. A great deal I have forgotten; but I remember that there were some very beautiful pieces of furniture, especially cabinets and bureaus, and portraits of his sisters as young girls with flowers and birds in their hands. He had brought a loom and set it up in one of the great square downstairs rooms; in another was his cot. Although the stairs were hard for him, he came up with us—"My mother's room: that is her portrait"—and on to the third floor where there was a lovely chamber filled with French Empire furniture and a carved delicate mantel.

"My sister uses this when she stays here. She has lived a great deal abroad."

On the wide brown wall boards of the unfinished rooms soldiers and children had written names, numbers, an illegible remark or two, nothing like that poignant note once pointed out to me on a Maine beam: "June 3 1862 today mother drowned all of Blacky's kittens." No, there was nothing like that. Our host stood below, after inviting us to climb to the fourth floor and up the little steep last stairs for a view from the roof. When we came down again to the third floor he had thought of something which might interest us. He had opened a chest and taken out a small patchwork quilt made for a child's bed or cradle. The pieces were all of silk or satin or brocade, now frayed and cracked here and there with age, but very brilliant and gay still.

He held it up, touching it quietly with his frail hands.

"My own aunt made that for me when I was a baby," he explained. "I like to remember that as a girl she danced with Lafayette."

Chapter 38

It WAS a fall day, I remember. At the Meadows the fire burned brightly in the big fireplace and an old-fashioned bouquet of autumn flowers on the mantel cascaded downward in scarlet vines against the white paint. There must have been a dozen people moving about from the tea table to the sofas and big chairs. The pointer had been sent to lie by the fire in the gun room. Everyone ate cake which turned out to be birthday cake, and talked.

On the way home in the early darkness with the autumn constellations overhead I had stories to tell. I had sat for some time talking with a man who had lived abroad for several years as a boy. Now he lived all by himself in an old red-brick house by a deserted mill in the woods. I knew the place. I had been there. I had seen the waterfall and the green and broken timbers, and the brook up which the beaver came. I had seen the huge slab of stone which was his doorstep, and the ashes of the shed which he had burned down and into which the mother flying squirrel had returned to die because her young were there. I knew that the deer were his neighbors and that he lived most of the winter on canned venison and venison mincemeat, that country delicacy. But the day we were taken to call, he was away, and it was with great pleasure that I talked with him now. He was a sort of Maine Thoreau, the type of educated and charming man which all through American history can now and then be come upon in some forest clearing.

He told me many stories of the woods which came up to his doors and windows. One, I particularly remember. One day he saw an eagle swoop to the ground and fly up with something in its talons. As it circled upwards into the air a curious thing happened. The great bird seemed to hesitate far overhead and then began slowly to spiral downwards again, nearer and nearer to the earth, and at last crashed forward onto the ground.

The watcher ran up in time to see a weasel slide away among the grasses. The eagle had bled to death from a severed artery in its throat, for somehow in the air the roles had been reversed and the prey had managed to reach upwards far enough to give the eagle its death wound and to descend safely again to the distant earth with its dying captor.

Then at some shift of chairs and guests I had talked with a man and his wife, returned not long ago from sixteen or seventeen years in South America. I heard something of the life there, but enjoyed still more an 1812 story of the old farm they had taken on a knoll extending out into a bay of one of the rivers. It is a lovely house on a little green peninsula, like a sunning lizard, very solitary, too, and no doubt more solitary a hundred and thirty years ago.

The story goes that the woman of the house was alone there one day when a British vessel came up the river foraging for food—for such cattle, sheep, and garden truck as they might commandeer from the river farms. She was all alone, but put on that oldest of stratagems by which the helpless insect imitates the stinging insect, the harmless snake the viper, and even such a thing as the cat bristles to pretend to a size she does not possess.

At any rate the woman pulled on her husband's trousers and old coat and snatched up a hat of his, and ran out across the barnyard and into the barn, in clear sight of the river. Creeping quickly back, she put on a different coat and a scarlet muffler and ran out of a different door and rang a bell loudly. From behind a wall she appeared again as though hurrying up from a field; in another hat and coat she once more left the house, priming a musket.

The pitiful ruse worked. The British vessel went on without stopping at a farm so bristling with farmers. Some other less resourceful and resolute household furnished provender that day, and no doubt the mistress of the knoll farm went back to her churning with a beating heart and brightened color, in a mood between laughter and tears.

Chapter 39

ONE OF THE outstanding features of pioneer life was and is its frequent isolation. I know of two cases myself where a family has been marooned without its men, and faced starvation waiting for their return. One case was on lonely Matinicus Rock where there is an old lighthouse, and the old stone keeper's-house, now abandoned, still stands looking out over the sea towards distant Monhegan and the Main.

The keeper and his family and assistants live a little farther down the slope towards the boathouse and the runway. There is no shelter at the Rock. If there is any sea running one cannot land a boat there. The place is only a few acres of tumbled slabs of stone between which grow wild angelica and other island weeds, shading the nests of a great colony of terns. The air is filled with these birds and their cries and their sharp-cut neat bodies slicing down towards one's head, while their pink beaks (which match their pink feet) snap to and fro like scissors. They are a violent pretty cloud of wings overhead to the stranger, but the lighthouse people grow very tired of them and their nests, and wish that a way might be found to keep them from fouling the cistern water on an island where there is no spring.

I have been on Matinicus Rock and climbed carefully over its difficult terrain to see a small colony of sea parrots which chose the most remote outpost of cliff to perch on. I have seen the fringes of its rockweed rising and falling in the wash, and heard the clear-cut slat of falling water when a passing whale blew a great spout like a narrow fountain. They told us how, about the time of the Civil War, a keeper had rowed ashore for provisions and was caught and held on the Main for twenty-seven days of gale, during which his twelve-year-old daughter took his place, tending the light all night through, and showing great courage and foresight in running out during the full terror of the first storm to rescue the chickens which were to stand between the family and starvation in the long days to follow.

That is a story of which Mrs. Cruickshank has written in her charming *Bird Islands Down East*, illustrated with photographs taken by her husband; but I heard it told before I read it in print. The other story of isolation is more anonymous, and the dreary little drama was played out in an old house on Westport Island which friends of ours have taken. If Matinicus Rock is almost like a wave shattered and frozen into granite far out to sea, Westport Island is a mere fringe of land in the Sheepscott River which has become detached from its shore. It lies far up from the sea in the tidal waters, with its farms and woodlands and coves. One still has to go to it by a ferry, pushed along a heavy cable by a capable power boat. There is still at the foot of the hill the old board giving the tariff for neat cattle, for ox teams, carriages, and sheep. The ferryman goes to his lunch at half-past eleven and returns at half-past twelve, and woe betide the man who wishes to cross the river while the ferryman eats. His motor horn will sound in vain, for long years have inured the ferryman to calm in the face of impatience.

Once on Westport Island, the road wanders for some miles to the small village at the far end. But the lane to our friends' house branches off through the woods, a mere vein of a road, dipping down over a stream which they have now dammed, and so coming out to cleared fields and two houses commanding a fine broad view down the river. There is a cove and a reef where the seals bark, and near the water the gray shingles of a ship's chandlery. Life came by the river in those days, and the big house is clapboarded on the two sides which might be seen from the water; but the humbler shingles would do for the lane to see. The place has wonderful cellars too, and fireplaces large and small. The sons of the present family catch lobsters, often cooked by the edge of the water where the stream enters the river and the two great mill wheels lie on the rock. The original mill was a shingle mill: once cedar shingles were made here for the West Indies trade. Farther down the river there is another gray chandler's shop, which, according to tradition, was usually kept by a woman living alone, who sat at the counter with a gun laid across her lap.

Now the story which they tell of this tall river-fronting house is for me dated only by the Revolution. The companion house had not been built at that time. The clearing stood alone, and its family lived alone; and when the man went to the war they were left quite alone there, locked in and barred by the forest.

Time passed, and the man did not return when he was expected. Had something happened to delay him, or had he been killed? There was no way to know. It was winter now, and the food in the kitchen was very low. There was no chance for a woman and little children to get more from the woods, and the deep snow barred them from their distant neighbors.

Every day they ate less and less, and then came a cold bright morning when the woman put the last of the corn meal before the fire and made the last johnnycake. There was nothing more to eat. The family stood about the table to say grace, and it must have been a desperate and poignant grace which was said. As one of the little girls raised her head, she saw through the window her father plodding across the snow dragging a heavily laden sled of provisions. And when all else about them has been forgotten, the tradition of that grace remains, as much a part of the house as the bricks of its chimneys and the wide boards of its floors.

Chapter 40

PERHAPS nothing is ever quite lost. But in Maine old things linger on more visibly than in many parts of the land. You may meet with the blacksmith, his Ford drawn up by the side of the road, his fire kindled in a metal barrel on a trailer and his hammer ringing against the iron of a horseshoe, while a horse stands patiently in the open barn door to be fitted. You pass the modern peddler with his tinware or his delivery truck opening out onto shelves of canned goods or dress goods. One we are very fond of advertises on the body of his car "Pain Oil" and "Salad Oil." The bull passes by in his own trailer, visiting the farms. There are still flails hung on a nail in the barn, still oxen to be seen plowing, or pulling their loads of hay; still old-fashioned furniture and parlor organs in the parlors, and many lamps burning in rooms which have never known electricity.

So it does not seem particularly curious that every year the Indians come to us selling baskets. Many things at the farm are kept in Indian baskets which must have been peddled at the same door fifty years ago. Nowadays they drive in cars, and the style of the baskets has changed subtly to meet the modern taste; but the fundamentals are all the same—the wide ash splints of the heavier baskets and, for the smaller ones, the edgings of sweet grass which only the Indians seem to know how to find.

The Maine Indians were always a rather peaceful people, often preyed upon by the Mohawks from what is now New York, who came over on raiding expeditions from time to time. We have become acquainted with several families of Old Town Indians. I am interested to notice that it is the wives who remember the Indian words for things which their husbands have forgotten. They are hard-working quiet women with a smiling look. They say little, but their husbands seem always to turn to them before making a decision. I remember a room in an Old Town house with sixty or seventy red-paint ax heads and fishing weights spread on the floor. It was a question as to whether we could buy a single piece. The man sat back on his heels, his fingers tapping unconsciously a drum tune on the floor boards. He was considering. No, he would not part with the curious ball of iron, shaped like a head. But perhaps a duplicate stone shell? But before he decided he glanced at his wife in the doorway. She did not speak, nor nod, nor smile; but a sense of "Yes" flowed from her like light, and he sold the shell-shaped fishline weight.

I remember another scene, not in Maine but in an Indian village on the lower St. Lawrence. The man had long thin mustaches and a watch chain strung across his open vest. He was a Montagnais, but his wife, the tall woman at the stove with a man's hat on her head (that was the old fashion with squaws all over the East) came from that very northernmost tribe of Indians, the fierce Nascapi, who so often war upon the Eskimos.

A member of our party wanted to buy for a museum the drum which the man had. I think he was willing. The hunting had been bad the year before, and he must soon be buying more supplies from the Hudson's Bay Company for the winter's trapping. The Montagnais, men and women and children, spend their summers in villages on the river; but in September they return to the northern forests and, breaking up into small family groups, hunt and trap all winter, living in tents.

So when the chance for a trade came the man hesitated. He spoke to his wife, this time in words, and she answered, speaking at some length, with an expressionless face. Her husband translated what she had said into Montagnais for the priest who was with us.

"They hunt alone," the father explained, turning towards us again. "She says that when night comes he plays upon the drum, and it is like the beating of her heart. She does not want him to sell it."

My closest acquaintance, however, is with an Indian woman long since in her grave beside her husband, Neptune. I was writing a book on the early Maine of 1817, just before the state broke off from Massachusetts to begin a separate existence. I was reading town histories and other simple local narratives, and among them was a little book published in 1860 or 1870 which mentioned an Indian woman named Molly Molasses who had once saved a white man from drowning, and who was considered as something of a prophetess, because she had foretold a great future for a newborn baby who became governor of the state in due course of time.

The name caught my fancy. Molly Molasses! Into my book she should go. It never occurred to me that within her own sphere she was an historical character with her own connections and associations, but later I was to receive a letter which startled me. It was from an elderly woman now living in the South. I have mislaid the letter, which told the story far better than I shall tell it. The writer was a white woman and had been born in Bangor where Molly Molasses was then living. Molly was a friend of the family's, and when the baby was born the Indian woman asked if she might be godmother. Her presents to her godchild were more than silver cups and leather Bibles. She gave the newborn girl a beautiful woven belt, and the power to curse and bless. The child knew only about the belt as she grew up. She was twelve years old before she learned what else had been given her.

At that time her family had a young dog, which one day leaped up on a neighboring child and scratched him with its claws. The child's father demanded that the dog should be shot, although all the children of both families begged for its life. But the man was overbearing—he was a member of the police force and something of a bully as well —and the dog's owner shot it rather than have trouble over the affair. Not content with issuing his order, the neighbor came into the house at suppertime to make sure that he had been obeyed. But there he went too far, had he but known it. Seeing the little girl red-eyed with tears at her place at the table, he began to make fun of her for crying over a dog. She jumped to her feet.

"As there is a God in heaven," she cried, "may I live to see you ruined and in tears!"

When the man had gone her mother scolded her.

"You must be careful what you say," she told the child. "You have the power to bless and curse, you know."

The girl had not known. She listened eagerly to her mother's account of her godmother's gift. When in a few months she saw the neighbor ruined and in tears, she believed in her own power. And all her life she has felt it within her—the Indian woman's gift, to curse or to bless.

I am continually fascinated by what interesting people live all about us. The world is a wider and more exciting place for holding in it a woman to whom Molly Molasses bequeathed her gift. Since reading the letter I have seen a portrait of Molly's daughter in a Bangor club, an Indian belle with beadwork ornaments and bright-colored flounces. And a year or two ago an Indian woman showed us Molly Molasses' cross—a French one, of silver with double arms as I remember it. The woman, who was her great-granddaughter, said that Molly Molasses had worn that cross to the day of her death; and it was touching to hold it in the palm of one's hand. But what was a silver cross inherited by a great-granddaughter to the gift she had given to her white godchild, the gift of power, the black magic and the white?

Chapter 41

IF ONE HAD three lovely daughters born on such a farm as ours, they might be named Sylvia, Echo, and Demeter. Their names would suggest the woodland, the rocky echo-haunted heights, and the sloping fields combined in these farms, where the wild and the tame are in continual inter-play like shadows of leafy branches in a wind.

Certainly the cows here have often met with deer and moose, and the late hay is filled with well beaten little paths of porcupines visiting the apple trees about the houses, and on the fall evenings one listens to make certain whether it is a fox or a farm dog yapping in the distance. The fox seems to impress the imagination of every countryside where he is common, and appears as Br'er Fox, or Reynard in his monk's gown, or the ghost foxes of Japan which can take the shape of beautiful women to beguile the lonely traveler.

Here there are no legends of foxes that I know of; but they do curious things and are noticed. Old Mr. and Mrs. Hardy looked out early one autumn morning and saw a big red fox sitting in the sunlight of the dooryard staring at their windows and lolling his tongue out and laughing.

"The impudence of him!" cried Mrs. Hardy indignant at the memory of it. "Walter went to get his shotgun, but before he could load it the fox went off, laughing at us still. I didn't like it, I tell you. He was so bold about it like we were nothing to be afraid of."

"Has one ever come so near the house before?" I asked.

Mrs. Hardy thought. "Once when the old black cat was alive—you know, the one who could open doors and knew when a setting hen wasn't on her eggs. Well, I remember once looking out and seeing the old cat coming up the road with a fox following along after her, about four-five feet behind. Every time the fox came up nearer, the old cat would turn round spitting terrible, and that fox would kind of draw back. But you know they dearly love cat flesh. I went out and waved my dishcloth, and Mr. Fox thought he'd better go off on his business."

Mr. Hardy spoke up from his big rocking chair with that air of slow deliberation which adds an importance to anything he says.

"Funny thing about foxes," he remarked meditatively. "They won't go near anything iron which a man has touched. I had a turkey once with a crooked foot, and she stole a nest at the edge of the woods. I found it, and I took out a chain—wagon trace, it was—and made a circle round the nest. But I was in a hurry to get back to dinner, and I didn't see to it that the ends quite met.

"Next morning I went to see how she was. She was gone, and every egg was broken and sucked. Only thing left was that crippled foot of hers. Fox had come right through the gap."

Last fall there was a fox in our neighborhood that screamed. "When the mists rise from the lake the foxes mate," the people hereabouts say. Walking by night down along the Heath, as our moor is locally called, we heard this screaming sound beyond us, and later were told that

Paul, the caretaker at the sawmill, had met a fox on the road at dusk and it had screamed at him. Paul is a French Canadian, who has almost forgotten his native tongue after long solitary residence among Yankee neighbors. But I feel sure that old memories must have wakened in his mind, and northern stories of haunted spirits stirred at the back of his thoughts.

I have seen foxes often here, and still more often followed their busy interweaving tracks in new-fallen snow, and smelt their odor like old grapes. But there were two little foxes which I became well acquainted with. I remember driving up to our friends', the Taggetts', house in the village on a May afternoon. The boys were then perhaps twelve and fourteen years old, and somewhere they had found or been given a pair of very young fox cubs. A fisherman whose dory had been followed home by a baby seal, perhaps deserted by its mother, had given them the seal. Elsewhere they had acquired a wire-haired fox terrier puppy, a kitten, and a pair of big Belgian rabbits. The green dooryard was a perfect scene of the mingling of the wild and tame. The little seal had been taken down that morning to the cove half a block away in a wheelbarrow for its day of swimming, but as usual it had grown hungry before it was called for again, and had flipper-flapped its way home along the concrete sidewalk, practically stopping traffic. I remember its fat baby face, its round eyes and its whiskers which twisted in corkscrews. Sue Taggett was coaxing it away from the flower border with a fish while the two little foxes with their pointed faces and big ears very large for their tiny bodies, dashed about through the tall grasses like excited demons. The puppy barked ecstatically, but it was the kitten which really played with the cubs, lying in wait for them, dashing out from ambush, to roll and scuffle with them on the warm earth. Seeing our amusement, the boys let out a big hare, which hopped about placidly, and then joined the sport by allowing the little foxes to chase it, and then chasing the cubs in turn, leaping over them in a great bound.

Suddenly there was a squeal of rage and a scuffle. A foxlet had smelled the fish which Neptune was eating. It had rushed upon the baby seal and had given it a sharp nip on the nose, seizing the piece of fish it coveted and running off into a thicket of grass to devour what it had stolen. Someone picked the culprit up by the scruff and cuffed it lightly.

"You ought to be ashamed! Poor Neptune!" The little seal looked upset and surprised, but forgot its troubles at the appearance of another herring.

The last time I saw either fox was some months later. Neptune had been returned to the sea. The kitten and puppy were living the immemorial lives of their kind; the rabbits were in a hutch. But the little foxes had been returned to the woods above Green Cove. I had walked down to see the Taggetts on their houseboat and had with me that big black pit-bull terrier called Bos'n who was for so long the household dog, the gentlest-hearted creature that ever drew breath—"an old dog saint," we used to call him—for all his warlike tradition. As Sue and I walked along the path by the edge of the Cove we saw something golden-red flitting towards us from the cliffs, frisking among the pines. It was the little vixen, now almost full-grown, who had heard Sue's voice and had come to meet her. I caught Bos'n by the collar. The pretty fox came up to us, rolling on the path and playing a little like a dog, a little like a cat, but with a charming elfin gayety which belongs to neither. When she reached us she came up to Bos'n, whom she had never seen before, and touched his nose with her delicate nose tip. He whined, bewildered and enchanted, and she played about us confidently. For that moment, she was the spirit of the August woods, harmless and fearless, at peace with itself, and neither wild nor tame, but something beyond either.

KATAHDIN WAS the sacred mountain of the Indians. No Indian was so hardy as to climb its holy cliffs. To the Indians it was the abode of the spirit Pamola, with the claws of an eagle, the body of a man, the head of a moose, and the eye of a wildcat. When the storm came howling through the forests and the thunder rolled among the mountaintops they believed that Pamola was in his great cave, stamping its stone floor with boulders fastened to his claws, while skeletons danced about the fire in the cavern's center.

But Pamola was partly like a man, and sometimes he stole a woman from the Indians and carried her off to his dark retreat. There is a story of such an Indian woman who grew lonely for her tribe and was allowed to return on a visit to them with her big fierce boy, and of how finally she broke her promise to tell no one who was the child's father, and so brought ruin upon them all.

Curiously enough, the people of Maine still have a very special feeling for Katahdin. It is loved and spoken of in a way no other mountain in Maine is. It is apart from others: its heights are greater, its waterfalls more magnificent, its lakes lie about it like the sky fallen and caught in the hollows. Still, people will tell you of the caribou herd which loved its tundras, the last in Maine, which some hunters, with the wicked selfishness of which they are but too capable, drove over a cliff, in one awful second blotting out for all others the pleasure of seeing caribou wandering on the bare mid-heights of Katahdin where was created for them their own Arctic Circle. Their bones and horns, I am told, may still be seen, like an old brushwood pile at the bottom of that fateful cliff. I cannot see why the government does not restock the mountain with half a dozen pair of caribou, protected by law, and let them again become part of that noble landscape, so that with the eagles they may bring back that sense of life welded to the scene, which adds so much to the delight of the onlooker.

Well, I have seen the northern lights of late October flame along Katahdin's brow, and drunk the fiercely cold and pure waters of its streams. But I have only heard at second hand the stories of the guide Roy who for so many years ran a camp by a pond half way up the mountain and in the evenings, pipe in hand, spun his yarns of Pamola before the fire.

One reads nothing of Pamola among the folk figures of America; but he is deeper-rooted than Paul Bunyan himself, and surely as interesting. They say that Roy knew all about his life and everything which happened to him, that people of all sorts sat enthralled by his stories which wove a spell about listeners for which they afterwards could never find words. There was, for instance, the trouble Pamola had the time he went to sleep in the sun and a porcupine crawled into his ear thinking that it was a burrow. That made a lot of trouble. And another time Pamola had all the fire wardens telephoning for the fire-fighting crews from as far off as the city of Bangor. That was the time when he sat down for a quiet pipe back of the mountain.

He didn't dream that with every puff the sky was gray with smoke. No, he hadn't meant to bother anyone.

And there was that other fall when he began to feel so lonely, and finally stole a middle-aged schoolteacher with glasses right out of her log cabin. There was a terrible fuss over the affair; and all the guides took their shotguns, and the state police came in on their motor cycles, and there was a great rumpus until they found her note, pinned to a pine tree with what may have been one of Pamola's hairs.

"Don't look for me. Am having a wonderful time. Will you please inform the Detroit school board that I will not be back?"

According to Roy there have been many changes in Pamola's life since then. He has become domesticated with a vengeance. From the camp it is possible to study the entrance of Pamola's famous cave through field glasses, and early next summer Roy began to make out curious white squares along the cliff beside it, seen especially on sunny days. They weren't always in the same pattern either; but there were always a lot of them, and they kind of moved when there was a wind. It was interesting to speculate on what they were. Roy wasn't quite sure until one fine late afternoon he saw Pamola himself come out with a Sears Roebuck perambulator and start pushing it up and down, up and down, on the sort of terrace in front of the cave.

Well! So Pamola had had a little blessing, had he? But it wasn't like Indian days with the papoose hung out on a bough like a Christmas stocking. This was a white baby. You could hear it holler when the wind was right, and it had to have its rides in the baby carriage every pleasant afternoon. That schoolteacher believed in fresh air. Roy could see that every now and then poor Pamola would get tired and want to go into the cave again, maybe to cook up a good storm. But she must have known how to manage him. After a moment, out he would pop, baby carriage and all, and start marching back and forth again. She wouldn't even let him have his storms for fear of keeping baby in. Not even at night for fear of disturbing baby's sleep. Pamola didn't have much fun that summer: no one could ever remember so much good weather. By the middle of July the streams had dried up and by August 1st the leaves were falling. But that schoolteacher was dead set against winter. Why, it wasn't until . . . And so the yarns went on. Roy knew just how Pamola felt about everything, and what he did. I rather think he used to meet him sometimes for a good talk on the sunny side of the mountain. Now if only someone would put back those caribou I'd think that Katahdin was a mountain well furnished with all that a mountain should have: beauty, solitude, a legend, and its own especial creatures, of which only it, of all the mountains in the country, was guardian.

Chapter 43

I HAVE A very charming friend who has gardenias every winter from a great plant slipped long ago from the first gardenia her first beau gave her to wear to her first dance. There must be an inheritance of gayety, prettiness, and lightness of touch in the family, for one day she told me a story of her grandmother, whom I am sure she is just like.

As a girl, grandmother lived in a small Maine town where her father was the minister. It was early spring—not mud time, but the time when the maples are in blossom and the apples are in bud. The village girls were in a great state of excitement because a young man of the place had returned for a visit to his parents after some years spent in the Sandwich Islands—or perhaps they were already called the Hawaiian Islands. He was said to have made a fortune. He was said to be thrillingly handsome. And then he was such a romantic figure! Few people had seen him yet, but it was known that he would be at church, and it was spring, and the young girls were in a frenzy, choosing their dresses and bonnets.

The sixteen-year-old daughter of the minister was as excited as anyone. I imagine more excited, but in an airy, merry fashion. And then her father spoiled it all by saying that she could not attend the morning service. She must stay at home and be nurse to the younger children. She was left there in her old house dress with bad little brothers and sisters, while all the other girls in town went by in their prettiest dresses looking like so many cats who have been lapping cream. She heard the church bells ringing across the new grass, and saw the lazy Sunday curls of smoke from the chimneys, and perhaps later she could even hear the sound of hymns slanting out from the open windows of the church. There the girls were, all singing their loudest, hoping to catch the eye of the young man, coquetting under their bonnet brims, or tilting their wicked little chins as though their thoughts were only on heaven; and here she was, indoors, in her old dress, wiping Betsy's nose and telling Asa not to eat buttons from the sewing basket!

The long service came at last to its end, and at the church door a bevy of townsfolk surrounded the wanderer, half neighbor, half stranger after these years of absence. Probably he saw a ring of pretty faces, heard a whole chorus of bird voices, was pierced by a battery of eyes peeping at him through their lashes.

And then he walked home under the spring-red maples with his papa and mama, and as he passed the minister's house there was a stir at an open window and between the white curtains a little figure appeared. Although she was going nowhere she had on the choicest of bonnets, and lace mitts were on the hands parting the curtains, and the face that looked out was smiling, above the prettiest of dresses.

"Hello, John Edwards!" the vision called. "Won't you marry me?"

His name was not John Edwards. But otherwise the story is true. And he married her.

Chapter 44

Humor on the farms usually goes back to some sort of
practical joke, played by Fate or by a human being; and
very often it has to do with the farm animals, since they
lend themselves readily to comedy. Sometimes the fun of
the scene is entirely unconscious. A friend working in her
garden was roused by the sound of an angry voice coming
down the country road, punctuated by loud whacks.

She looked up to see a cow followed by a thin elderly
woman. The cow was placidly chewing something which
hung in delicate fringes from her mouth. The woman who
followed, staff in hand, was less placid.

"Going into the graveyard!" *Whack.* "I'll teach you!"
Whack. "How dared you go"—*whack*—"and eat"—*whack*—
"the columbine off"—*whack*—"Euphelia's grave?"

Some New England writer has named the cow "the
horned torment." Yesterday for the third day in succession
we called in to our neighbor's wife at the kitchen door,
"One of your cows is out on the road by the Heath!" and
yesterday she replied grimly: "Drat that cow! We'll beef
her." No Maine cow does herself any good by being too
sedulous to find gaps in stone walls or sagging wires.

But the real low comedian of the farm is probably the
pig. Mrs. Hardy told us a story from the past, without
names, as most of her stories are told.

One of the farmers of the last generation came home by night, having cheered himself with friends a little too deeply. His wife heard the wheels of his buggy and came to the door with the lamp just as her husband walked up the path holding a pig in his arms. At the steps the pig gave a well timed wiggle, slipped from his grasp, and tore into the clump of lilac bushes by the door, upsetting the white hen who had her nest there. Out came biddy, flapping and clucking wildly as she made off; out ran the wife to head off the little pig.

"Let it alone! Let it alone!" shouted the farmer. "Damn a pig with wings!"

Chapter 45

It was in mid-July when each of our mailboxes of the "rural route boxholder-local" was found to contain a bright green newspaper "published in the interest of education" with cuts of whales and descriptions of Colossus, the fifty-five-foot finback who was to appear for two days at the end of the week at the Rockland railroad siding in "his especially constructed bridge steel car." In other articles (for a good deal appeared about whales, from Jonah's down) Colossus was referred to as the "Captive Whale." And to make the "railroad show" still more exciting there were promises of a flea circus and an account of the training of fleas and of their intelligence and temperaments.

Wild horses could not have kept me from Rockland on the appointed day; certainly drizzle and fog were not enough to discourage me. Henry was not interested, rain or shine; but I found a friend to go with me, and we drove off, with our headlights on, going slowly through the hollows where the white fog lies like water, and slowly around the curves where the road shows drenched and glistening. Slowly as we drove, we were too early for our appointment with Colossus.

We inquired our way to the small gray station, under whose eaves a few families were waiting partially shielded by umbrellas. Another group or two bided their time in parked cars that shone dully in the wet grayness of the day. Freight cars stood dejectedly on their sidings, and at some distance an engine puffed and panted. Down one dull street there was a narrow glimpse of gray harbor water.

The roustabouts were still busy about the bridge steel car, whose sides opened in the center and parted, the upper halves to form an awning and the lower halves to form a walk about Colossus. The gangplank stairs had been let down, and five or six wet and ragged little boys were waiting for the moment when they might ascend, free if they could only find a grown-up to attach themselves to. With that sparrowlike awareness of street children they knew already all the figures: the number of tons Colossus weighed, the number of feet he measured from nose tip to fluke.

Waiting there in the rain, we grew uneasy. It was past the time given in our green newspaper for the show to open, and we were expected home for tea. Resolutely we mounted the gangway to the car, and unhitched the rope across the entrance. An elderly man in a captain's uniform —and his speech and carriage made me think that he *had* spent fifty-six years on New Bedford whaling ships as "The Whale Journal" claimed—was willing to take our dimes. He started to explain Colossus to us, but just then the distraught manager bore down upon us, the bright little dimes were taken from the captain's seamed palm, and we were hustled down the gangway.

But we had seen all. We had seen Colossus lying prone, his tail bolted together with an iron bar where at some time it had split apart; we had seen the rents in his gray sides from which the rock salt with which he was stuffed spilled a little, though he had been darned together with rope as thick as a painter; we had seen the long slits about the head like a car's radiator, and the big mouth "capable of swallowing a man."

So, satisfied, we descended again to the ground and turned to a car at right angles to "Colossus." It was much smaller and held "Jolly Stella," according to a new sign, though the old legend along the car itself still spoke of "Jolly Jumbo, the largest hog in the world."

There was no objection to our seeing Stella. She was as ready for visitors as she ever would be. We took out our dimes again and gathered up two little boys in tow ("children under twelve free with adults"), and we all went to see Jolly Stella. And she was jolly, she was as alive as Colossus was dead. She lay shining-pink, almost hairless, and enormous in a perfectly clean pen. When she heard our footsteps she opened one eye sleepily above her vast smiling jowl and closed it again. It did you good to look at anything so large, so healthy, and so sleepy. It warmed the gray cold day, the gray dead whale, the cindery air above the siding.

No one seemed to know a thing about the flea circus, with its fleas, some cooperative and some noncooperative. But we could let that go. We had seen a real survival of those little nineteenth century shows, where an elephant or a pair of lions, an ostrich or a giraffe found their way from New England town to town, their manager always assuring the populace that here was no ungodly "show," no slightest relative to the theater and its wickedness, but merely an educational exhibit, clarifying for the young some passage of the Bible, practically a living paragraph from the concordat.

And so, in the rain, we had seen one of these exhibits,

precursors of Barnum & Bailey, of Ringling and the other vast circuses, and now a survival, lingering on. I wonder at how many other farms the "Whale Journal" has been kept, with its photographs of modern whaling, and its old prints from the days of the New Bedford "sleigh rides." Here are some of the headlines:

"Whale Last Prehistoric Animal." "Killer Whale Tiger of the Seas." "Captain Barnett Spins Yarn London Would Envy." "Whale Would Drown If Kept Down." "Jonah Story True, Claims Negro Mammy."

I glance over the four exciting pages, and come to the account of a James Bartley of the vessel *Star of the East*, who in February, 1891, off the Falkland Islands was cut out unconscious but alive from the body of a bull whale. He remembered having been thrown high into the air from the whaleboat, and having heard a sound like the rumbling of a train "going at full speed"; he remembered darkness, slime, heat, and compression. He remembered horror, and then—no more! I hope other readers will be as glad as I am to know that after hovering between life and death for two weeks, sipping brandy, "he recovered sufficiently to carry on his duties, [but] his skin never regained its natural appearance. It retained a deathly white pallor."

Can life on a farm be dull, when any morning something like this may appear in the mailbox?

Chapter 46

UNTIL LAST YEAR we had a very small clapboarded station at our flag stop. The tracks run here between two hills, with the road making a sharp U down to and over them. The steel has the shine of water. It might be a stream, for the place looks like a stream bed; but there is no water here.

The station had two rooms—a little baggage room and a little waiting room which held a coal stove and had a narrow wooden bench running along three sides. Before the days of the automobile, I imagine, it was used more than it has been in late years. When I knew it, it was most often used by tramps who were sent there by kindly villagers, as there is no police station in the town where a tramp may spend the night.

"Just go down the next road to the right—a short mile— to the railroad station. You'll find a stove and coal, and I guess you can fix yourself up. The door's open."

As we drove by, it was not unusual to see smoke rising from the stovepipe and a ragged figure taking the sun on the south side of the building. The nearest farm often raised vegetables in the field sloping upwards south of the station. The tramp could find a few potatoes or a mess of beans, nor was it grudged him. I suspect that if he asked at the neighboring doors he was given bread, milk, and eggs. The country people are generous to others. A share of their produce they are willing to give to any applicant.

One fall, a tramp stayed at the station for two or three weeks. The place was secluded, out of the wind—a rural solitude, yes, but a solitude shaken at times by the familiar passing of little trains, by the shout of the conductor, "All aboard."

No one troubled him, and he troubled no one. We were sorry when the accustomed trail of smoke no longer drifted from the stovepipe and we knew that he had gone on.

Now the station too has been torn down. We have only a platform, a flag and a pole to put it in, and two lanterns; and if there are still tramps they have to go on to larger and perhaps less kindly villages. I have never heard of any difficulty with these modern tramps. They are not like the fierce and moody men who roamed the country after the Civil War, demanding food and lodging at the doors of lonely farms. When one reads the roster of the Civil War the number of men who went to it from our village is almost frightening. There are scarcely as many men now in the whole township. So often they never returned, but died in southern cornfields and by shallow brown streams; or they felt their ties with home loosened and went West. Old cellar holes guarded only by the lilacs, sightless gray farms rotting back to the earth are the monuments here of the Civil War. I can find out so little about it in the talk of the people. At the Hardys' farm they used to husk their corn by rubbing the ears across a bayonet fastened over a bucket. Mrs. Hardy's older brother had brought it back with him from the war. In another house I know, someone wrote with a diamond, on a pane of glass in the window at the end of the upstairs hall, a name and a date —"aged seventeen, gone to the war." Perhaps the boy's father and mother stood at that window and watched him trudging down the road, turning back to wave. We have a wonderful rug too, a hooked rug. A charger with flaring nostrils and hoofs far spread gallops across it, riderless, but saddled and bridled. The rug is all in shades of brown, black, and gray except for the red nostrils of the horse and the red and blue saddlecloth. The moment he saw it, Henry said, "That is the wool from a Union officer's uniform." In such small haphazard ways do great events trickle down through the years.

But a neighbor who had been brought up near Hamilton once told me about a tramp of the time after the Civil War. She was quite old, and this had happened to her aunt, who had been left alone for a few days on a farm with only her young daughter while her husband was away on some matter of business.

"Don't let any strangers into the house," he warned her. "Good-by. I'll be back as soon as I can."

Towards dusk on the first afternoon a tramp appeared at the kitchen door demanding food and a bed for the night. He was truculent when the woman told him that she would give him food but wouldn't take him in. He ate what he was given on the steps; but when he left he did not thank her. He looked at her and said:

"You'll be sorry for this."

She and her daughter watched uneasily as he went off down the road.

Before going to bed they locked up the farm with unusual care; but no one tried the doors or pushed upwards on the old window sashes during the night. It was the most dreaded of all farm visitors which broke in upon their sleep—fire. They woke to find the house burning in two places, and barely got out of it alive, running in their nightgowns up the stony road to the nearest neighbor's. The house of course was burned to the ground, and I suppose the man watched for a while from some field corner and then slipped off to put a few miles between him and his work before dawn.

Chapter 47

ONE DAY we went to an auction at a big house overlooking the river. No one had died. The people had not
even failed, but they had decided to sell off the things
which they didn't want. As the wife said to us, they were
"things not good enough to keep, but too good to throw
away." The day was pleasant. As usual, auctioneer, assistants, and buyers were grouped on chairs and benches in
the sunny angle between the kitchen and the open stable
door. There was none of that poignancy I have known, of
the threaded needle stuck through the spool of thread in
the saucer ready for someone to use who never again was
to use needle and thread. There was no murmur of some
friend behind us, "Oh, I do hope her clothes won't be
sold." No, here everything was cheerful: the attic was
holding the auction.

I can remember one man sat astride the big yarn wheel,
and the auctioneer called out to him, "Hey, you've got it
in reverse!" Three ladies with their knitting and packages
rose from a four-poster bed when it was time to put it up
with all the agitation and flutter of hens disturbed in their
dust baths under a hedge. There was a little boy, too, who
started each bid at ten cents. At last the auctioneer with

a kindly glance knocked down a stuffed owl to him at his first bid, and I remember the look on his face as he went to get his prize like one in a dream.

Although we didn't buy anything, I retain a very happy memory of the morning. In the barn there were half a dozen large framed pictures against the plows and carriage wheels: Beatrice Cenci, I am sure, and Landseer's Stag and The Princes in the Tower and a charcoal drawing of a negro boy done with considerable skill.

The mistress of the place saw us looking at the picture and stopped beside us.

"My uncle did that," she said. "It was Joe Dime's boy."

She saw that the name meant nothing to us.

"Joe Dime," she repeated. "He was the only negro in town in those days. One of the men brought him back after the Civil War. They say he paid a dime for him. Anyway he lived here in a little house down the road. He worked very hard. When his wife went insane and was taken to the Asylum he paid three dollars a week towards her upkeep because he didn't want to take charity. He used to work for my father. In those days this land paid for itself and the people lived well. My father had two brickyards down on the river and sent his bricks off up and down the coast. Then here he kept a hundred head of cattle, and back of the farm he had a sawmill. There was money in Maine then.

"Well, Joe Dime used to work at the brickyards, and one day my brother looked into his lunch pail and saw that he had only a piece of dry bread in it. His wife had been sent away. So Brother told my mother, and after that she always had a full lunch pail ready for Joe, waiting at the kitchen door. Everyone liked and respected him.

When he was over forty he went to school here with the little children to learn his letters. He said he wanted to be able to read the Bible, and he kept at it until he could read it. He lived to be very old, and when he died some of the most important men in the town asked to be his pall-bearers. They wanted to show their respect for him. Yes, everyone liked Joe Dime."

She moved away to speak to others, and we were left looking at the portrait of Joe Dime's son. I forgot to ask what happened to him. It was Joe Dime who seemed to matter.

Chapter 48

Aɴʏ ʜᴇʀᴍɪᴛ touches the imagination of the gregarious
normal human being. We all have our hermit moments,
and a man who goes to live by himself stirs our wonder and
interest and a hidden sympathy in some part of our na-
tures. I once met a pleasant German hermit at Palm
Springs, California, in the old days before Hollywood discovered the spot. He lived by the stream in the cañon
among the wild palms, and he had written little notices
asking people not to kill rattlesnakes if they should come
upon them: they were innocent creatures, seeking to
harm no one. And in Arizona there was a peripatetic hermit with a great beard who came through the country once
a year with a throng of dogs, some dogs pulling the cart
in which the man sat, others following behind it fastened
by cords, and two or three little dogs sitting with their
master in the light wagon riding through deserts and across
arid ranges.

I have been told too of a very disagreeable and sus-
picious hermit who used to live in the woods of New
Hampshire. It is rather terrible to think of the sufferings
of a timid hermit; and this man must have been very timid,
for he had arranged a pit set with knives by his door, and
had had scythes mortised into his chimney-mouth, as pro-
tection from intruders.

The hermit of Eagle Island was altogether different. I heard of him from one who used to see him as a child when her family visited the island for picnics. There had originally been two or three houses on the place; but the families had moved away, and only one old house and barn were left standing among the fields beyond the woods where the blue herons have their allegorical nests. At the other end of the island was the small cliff-hung harbor where my friend's family moored their boat, in a narrow inlet.

During their first visits they were not aware that any other human being shared the island with them; but after a while they made out a figure watching them from behind a screen of trees. If they approached, the figure withdrew. The man had lived so long alone that he was desperately shy, but interested as a deer might be in the goings and comings of strangers. It was the mother of the family who suggested that they might leave out sandwiches, a cup of coffee, and a banana when they went for their stroll about the heronry; and when they came back the food was gone. Bit by bit, they gained the hermit's confidence. Slowly he showed himself more openly; at last came the day when he would sit with them, though still with an air of arrested flight. They learned that he owned the island now and lived here winter and summer without so much as a cat or dog to share his solitude. He caught fish and, for the rest, drank a gruel of cornmeal stirred in water. On this Spartan diet he had lived for years.

In due course of time the picnickers bought the island. I asked what the hermit did then, expecting to hear that he had gone on living in the gray house to which he was accustomed. But no, by no means! he used the money to go to New Bedford, and there he worked as a sailmaker, accustoming himself once more to human ways.

"And, oh, yes," my friend added, "he was very fond of reading, books and magazines. Particularly, the *Atlantic*. Father used to send him his copy every month."

Chapter 49

THERE LIVED some years ago in a neighboring town a
solitary woman, who they say "wrote." No one seems to
have the least idea what she wrote, but the memory of
desk, ink, and pen clings to her story. As she got on in
years she made herself a shroud, to have on hand for her
burial, if she should sometime be taken suddenly ill.

Not long after the shroud was finished and folded away
in tissue paper in a lower bureau drawer there was a spell
of very hot weather. I imagine that the clothes of the period were tight and very uncomfortable in the heat. It
occurred to the lady that the shroud would be loose and
easy to wear in the house during the hot spell, and could
be put to some use before it took on its grimmer duties.
The experiment was a complete success. The shroud, made
like a loose white wrapper with wide sleeves and many
pleats, proved very comfortable. She began to appear in
her garden in it on hot afternoons. Finally she wore it
when riding horseback. She discovered that there was
nothing like a shroud for real comfort, and in summer she
was rarely to be seen in anything else. She wore out shroud
after shroud, and when she finally died the neighbors had
to make one for her, as there wasn't a shroud in the house
fit to be used.

Chapter 50

OUR COUNTRY NEWSPAPER is published once a week. It has eight pages, largely filled with local news. On the front page there may be some mention of national events, an editorial, Republican and sectional in policy, a column devoted to state happenings, and then the editors turn frankly to interests nearer home. Of course any neighborhood event is headlined, though sometimes with curious restraint, as when a fatal accident with a strong appearance of murder was noted under the simple words, "Unfortunate Occurrence at Taylors Springs." A letter from a local boy in Italy or the South Seas is very welcome. There may be the digest of a lecture or the account of a club meeting or of a golden wedding celebration. The names of all visitors to the Old People's Home are boxed, and the day of their visit noted. Then for several pages the news of the surrounding countryside is given. Each village has its own recorder, and in dull weeks even a call made on a Sunday afternoon to another farm a mile down the road may find the immortality of print. The items often absorb our attention because of the given names. Many names in New England seem to have suffered a curious change. They remind the hearer of ones he has come across before; but strange *i*'s have appeared, or syllables have been added or subtracted, so that the mind is confused as though somehow the name itself had been left out in the rain, and its pattern had "run." These local and homespun names are sometimes generations-old in a family; but their interest is added to by newer ones, picked up from the movies or other sources. I once asked someone in the family how a baby girl had come by her name, and was told that the young mother had taken it from a prize cow at the fair.

Speaking of babies, reminds me that we always look at the notes from the new hospital with interest, waiting for the enigmatic announcement which closes the list nearly every week. "To Mr. and Mrs. So-and-so, on such-and-such a date, a boy." "To Mr. and Mrs. So-and-so, on such-and-such a date, a boy." "To Mr. and Mrs. So-and-so on such-and-such a date, a girl." "To Mr. and Mrs. So-and-so, on such-and-such a date, *a baby*."

Now what do they mean by that?

Worth reading as the entire paper is, the essence of its New England quality appears most strongly in the Personal and Lost and Found Columns at the back. Among the notices of writing paper marked with one's name, cordwood, cottages, and cows for sale, beagle hounds and heifers strayed, and help wanted, there are usually some highly personal lines. Here you will find someone advertising for "a housekeeper who won't bite a man's head off, and knows how to mind her own business." Here a shotgun is offered in exchange for chickens, and (so that you may know that there is nothing wrong with the gun) the advertiser adds, "Reason for selling, rheumatism." Another week we find a sharp warning: "The person who took a lawnmower out of my barn last Saturday afternoon has one more chance to return it. The party was seen taking it." (I wonder if he really was. Or was that term "party" used to cover up the owner's ignorance as to even the sex of the culprit?)

But up to the moment of writing our favorite notice appeared over the name of a Taniscot grocer in this summer of labor shortage, and is a model of forthrightness and brevity.

"Wanted: Two boys the size of men to do the work of a pair of horses."

Chapter 51

ONE JUNE we felt that we should have more animal life on the farm, so we called on Lambert Bremen and borrowed a lamb from his flock to keep for the summer. I had memories of a black lamb which I had once seen in a Nova Scotian village, with a red bow on its neck, following its little-girl mistress to the post office like an animated verse from a school reader. Our older daughter, Margaret, who from earliest childhood has been the wild strawberry picker among us, was at camp but we had a little girl not at camp, and now would have a lamb. I insisted on a ewe, which could be returned without fear of the autumn butchering (it is pronounced "bootchering" with us). Unfortunately all the lambs had been born rather early that year. The lamb which was finally forced into the back of our car seemed rather large and strong to me, but Catherine greeted her with enthusiasm at our door and named her Blanche, with a sweeping Eve-like assurance.

All summer Blanche was a part of the farm life, but such a part! She was stupid, dull, and greedy. She felt no impulse to play or to follow her little-girl mistress or anyone else anywhere. I spent hours taking ticks from her fleece and dropping them into a tomato can filled with kerosene, but though Blanche throve amazingly she showed neither character nor affection. The only place one could be sure

[171]

to find her was at the tea table under the apple trees at four o'clock in the afternoon; and there she baaed, nagging persistently, ready to eat everything she was given with small sidewise twists of her narrow jaw. In fact one afternoon, when three unknown ladies came to interview Henry and the tray arrived while we were all in the herb garden, Blanche did not wait to be given her treat but reached up and took it for herself—not only her share, but everybody's else as well.

I had once imagined that Blanche's future fate would be a matter of great concern to me; but such wasn't the case. When she was finally returned I didn't care what might happen to her; I forgot all my plans for mittens and socks to be knitted from her wool. In fact Blanche was not *simpatica*. It was with Catherine, then about five, that my real sympathy lay when one dull afternoon I saw that enterprising little-girl mistress chasing her pet around the corner of the house with a broom.

"Catherine!" I cried with hypocritical reproof. "What are you doing to Blanche?"

Catherine looked me in the eye.

"I'm trying to make her *do* something, Mother."

I'm sure a run would have done Blanche good, but I played the mother's monotonous part and stopped the poor attempt at sport.

The pair of lambs that Mrs. Hardy once told us about were very different. They had been raised on the bottle, never having known a mother, and were very fat. But the little male insisted upon running with the hounds. The first time, it went with them only a little way into the woods and came back by itself; the second time, it went clear across the neck and someone "hitched" it. Mrs.

Hardy's father could hear it bleating, and the hounds led him straight to the right farm when he drove off to find the runaway. The lamb did the same thing another two or three times, and finally old Mr. Hardy decided he would have to sell it, much as he hated to. It was such a lively creature, but it made too much trouble. A lamb ought to behave like a lamb and not like a hound dog.

Chapter 52

Grace's mother was not the only country girl who was loved by a young man from the town, against the wishes of his family. There was hereabouts in the middle of the last century a very hot-tempered young man of good connections whose people objected to his marriage to a farmer's daughter. Apparently a good deal was said about the family name, and in a rage he declared that he'd drag the family name in the dirt. He made a career of doing so—one suspects it must have been a congenial task, as he entered into it so whole-heartedly. He gave up his gentle farm girl indeed, and left town. Now he was heard of in one city, now in another, drinking and merrymaking; now he was traveling through Ireland earning his night's lodging by playing on a fiddle. He was rarely sober; he knew none of the people of whom his family would have approved.

At last he returned to his native town with a wife and a string of children and took a small house a block or two away from his brother's mansion. While his brother played the village man of affairs, our disappointed lover played the ne'er-do-well. Somewhere in the picture he seems to have lost his family, for as an elderly man he lived at the inn alone. All week he was drunk and disreputable, but every Saturday with the greatest punctilio he sobered up, and every Sunday he appeared, correct and dressed in a fine broadcloth coat with brass buttons, well brushed to match his polished shoes. All day he might be seen, a distinguished figure, at morning church service, or walking along the village streets; but every Monday the broadcloth coat, the polished shoes, and the upright carriage were laid aside, and he returned to his lifelong occupation of shaming his relatives.

It must have been on a Sunday that he once hired a carriage and drove out to the farm where the sweetheart of his youth had lived. She had never married. In fact she had died of love, the neighbors said, wasting away probably from the tuberculosis so common in those days. He walked across the hayfields to see her grave in the family lot in a fence corner under a pair of maples. There was her stone, with her name and age on it—so young she must have seemed to the elderly man bowing over to read the words—and there, too, was her little epitaph, surely chosen by herself, worn and infinitely touching:

"Semper fidelis."

What did he think, standing there? Another oft-used phrase, still capable of crying out, comes to mind: "I have been faithful to thee, Cynara! in my fashion."

Some years later he died in his lonely room, having thoroughly realized his life's ambition.

Chapter 53

Y EAR BY YEAR, if you live in the same place and listen and feel the life of the community, your knowledge grows imperceptibly richer and truer. In this neighborhood the same families have lived in the same farmhouses for generations. They know pretty well what to expect from themselves and from their neighbors. No man or woman is quite a separate individual; each is one more fruit appearing on a tree of a recognized stock. True, the person may prove a sport, going back to some minor strain in the family; but usually each follows a more or less recognized pattern of life and character.

Recently while Grace has been ill, Laura Sherman has been helping us. Every afternoon we drive down to the gray Sherman farm under the elms for her, or she walks up the lane if the day is fine. Though she has been out of bed since four in the morning, her blue eyes are bright and she sings as she goes about her work of getting dinner. Her voice is particularly true and sweet, and she often sings oldfashioned sentimental songs of forty or fifty years ago which her mother-in-law has taught her.

"We like to sing down at our place," she says. "Often of an evening, after the work is done, we have a regular concert. Father Sherman sings bass, and Norman takes the tenor; Mother Sherman sings alto, and I'm the soprano. Oh, we have grand times. And Donald (he's four) tries to sing too, with his little voice, and the baby knocks his spoon against the table leg. I guess Norman wouldn't have married a girl who couldn't sing." And I hear her clear phrase of melody weaving from the pantry or the shed as she moves about.

The other day Laura happened to begin talking about Father Sherman's mother, long ago dead and buried in the farm graveyard where so many red roses blossom in June. I should like a slip from one of those bushes, but I am a little superstitious and do not quite dare ask any gift from the dead. You know you must never burn wood from a tree which has been struck by lightning or has grown in a graveyard; and though our neighbors, the Hills, are less superstitious than we are and last summer cut into cordwood the broken half of the oak which was split by lightning along their stone wall, I dare not follow their emancipated example and take any token from a grave.

But Laura's tale was not of death but of living, of old Mrs. Sherman as she had been fifty and sixty years ago. As a young girl she had been married to a man twenty-five years older, whose teeth were all double—a thing not very noticeable to the observer, but one which gave him great strength in biting through a nutshell or in splitting a bone for its marrow.

When his eldest boy, the present Father Sherman, was fourteen, this man died, leaving his young wife with six little children to bring up. Only one was of working age— still a child, we should now think, but he and his mother counted him as a man. He took over the farm and paid the taxes on it. He worked out, chopping wood for his neighbors at twenty-five cents a day or more rarely, fifty cents.

When he came home at night he milked eight cows and did the farm chores, sometimes sawing ice until midnight by lantern light, or splitting his own wood.

Meanwhile his mother was working as resolutely as he. The grocer came once a week, and she paid for what the seven of them needed with her spinning and weaving. To save her son the extra work of cutting more wood than actually must be had, she did her cooking and baking in the morning with the breakfast fire, which she then let go out, going upstairs into the spinning room on the south side of the house. I don't know if there was a fireplace or stove in that room to take the worst of the chill from the air; but cold it must have been. There she worked until the shadow of the windowpane on the sill warned her that the sun was going down and it was time for her to rebuild the kitchen fire. Once a week the neighboring women met in one kitchen or another to knit together. They would establish a working rhythm by repeating,

> "Little canoodle,
> Big canoodle,
> Take out your canoodle,
> Let me see your canoodle,
> Compare your canoodle with mine."

"Canoodle" apparently meant the knitting needle. One wonders from what foreign or forgotten word it came. Apparently the women's work rhymes in Maine were all of this primitive sort, for years ago Mrs. Hardy gave me the weaving rhyme:

> 'Tis one,
> 'Tain't one,
> 'Twill be one by-'n'-by.

At the end of the day's knitting the work of all the women was laid on the hostess's bed to be compared and appraised, and invariably Mrs. Sherman's was the best. The next time Henry and I were at our neighbors', Laura brought out some of old Mrs. Sherman's work for us to see. There was a tablecloth of linen made from her own flax. Father Sherman remembered how his father had planted the seed "before dawn, or it wouldn't have bloomed," and he described to us all the process of rotting the stems and getting the fibers out for spinning the linen thread. Then Laura sent Donald into the bedroom for the old blanket on his bed, also his great-grandmother's work. It was worn very soft and thin with the years, but the rose, orange, and black border seemed not to have faded.

Mr. Sherman handled it gently.

"That was sumac dye," he explained, pointing to the rose stripe; "and that's sweet-apple wood, and the black's from dark indigo. Oh, she could do anything, my mother. I never can remember seeing her without some work in her hands."

Epilogue

Work well done and bearing fruit has always given me satisfaction; but for joy, oh, for joy, give me the unexpected unearned gift, the sudden patch of wild mountain cranberries planted by no hand, but hiding its red light berries in nests of moss under the tendrils, like candy eggs in a child's Easter-egg hunt; give me the sudden unasked circling of an eagle with the sunlight blazing on white head and widespread tail; give me the unexpected gesture of a child, or the story blooming from the midst of talk. These are the things which quicken my sense of the bounty of living, of its infinite touching variations.

So I have gathered together these stories which were all told me by neighbors. Some of the tales may have strayed from truth and been shaped into folklore. A man only last night assured me that his old guide on Katahdin told him that the caribou moved away of their own accord north into Canada, swimming, I suppose, the wide St. Lawrence, disappearing towards the Arctic. But a friend earlier told me of the sumaclike branched horns of the caribou which he had seen at the bottom of the Katahdin cliffs. So with all of these stories: I cannot vouch for them. I can only say that I heard them with my own ears, some once, some many times, and wrote them down exactly as I heard them, because it seemed to me that a gathering of many stories from one focus has a certain value in giving the emotional background of a locality. And if Americans are to become really at home in America it must be through the devotion of many people for many small, deeply loved places. The field by the sea, the single mountain peak seen from a man's door, the island of trees and farm buildings in the western wheat, must be sung and painted and praised until each takes on the gentleness of the thing long loved, and becomes an unconscious part of us and we of it. For we are not yet at ease with our land, and it is restive and often sullen with us, like a horse which has been roughly broken to riding, and is left frequently standing uncared for in the sleet.